How free and open software is changing
the world

The Daemon, the Gnu, and the Penguin

Peter H. Salus

Title: The Daemon, the Gnu, and the Penguin
Author: Peter H. Salus
Editor: Jeremy C. Reed
Publisher: Reed Media Services

ISBN 978-0-9790342-3-7

For Mary

Contents

Excurses

The Daemon, the Gnu, and the Penguin

Thanks

I need to thank several hundred folks for their contributions to this work.

First, Mike O'Dell, who has shown confidence in my work for just over 20 years, and Pamela Jones, who has permitted me access to Groklaw since 2003; second, the many who have permitted me to interview them and ask annoying questions; third, the over 400 individuals, many pseudonymous or anonymous, who have commented on my work-in-progress; and, finally, my "victims" in Denmark, Finland, the Netherlands, Sweden, the UK, Brazil, Chile and at USENIX, SANE, the KWLUG, the HLUG, and Penguicon.

Like UNIX and Linux, this work has benefited from the open process. My thanks to Dennis Ritchie, Ken Thompson, Brian Kernighan, Doug McIlroy, Ted Dolotta, Richard Stallman, Linus Torvalds, Andy Tanenbaum, Rick Adams, Rob Kolstad, Mike Padlipsky, and Lou Katz are embodied in these pages.

Peter H. Salus
Toronto, 2008

The Daemon, the Gnu, and the Penguin

Foreword

I do not remember the first time that I met Peter Salus. No doubt this is a failing on my part, for if there is one person who is unforgettable, it is Peter.

Former university professor, former Executive Director of USENIX, former Vice President of the Free Software Foundation, author of many books and articles, and generally regarded as "The Historian of Unix", Peter has done more to relate the history of Unix and the Internet, explaining where and how they derived than any other person. And well he should, since he was there during much of this period, and in his own inimitable way helped to nudge developments along.

I remember the days that I was the chair of the Awards Committee for USENIX. We were chartered to give out a Lifetime Achievement Award. One of the criteria for the award was to recognize someone who had given much to the Unix community, yet had not otherwise received a lot of past recognition. At least twice Peter reached into his wealth of Unix history and suggested nominees who eventually were elected to receive the award. Other times Peter successfully argued against some potential candidates. His integrity is without bounds.

In this book he reaches back into the early days of computing, showing that even in "pre-UNIX" days there was freely available software, and rapidly moves forward to the Free Software movement of today, drawing analogies and linkages from various aspects of economics and life.

Peter's book reads as if he is standing (maybe sitting) in front of you. If you are expecting a calm, ordered flow through this entire history, you will be disappointed in that aspect ... but I do not think you will be disappointed in the book itself. On the other hand, how could there be a ordered flow to a topic that had so many parallel threads and interleaved dependencies? Peter is a story-teller (as am I), but he is a story-teller with a deep set of facts and notes that back up his stories and show how the long, strange trip of Free Software came about, and what it means for the future.

Why the future? While the world of closed-source, proprietary software may never completely go away, enough has happened to show that closed-source software can not meet the demands of today's global society in terms of flexibility, longevity, and a price that people who can barely afford 100–200 U.S. dollar computers can pay. Rather than have these people who earn the equivalent of one to two U.S. dollars a day *pirate* software, perhaps it is better to have them write new software and contribute their efforts to the world's economy. This means that these people are not given code as a hand-out, instead they become part of the Free Software Community, standing shoulder to shoulder with other programmers around the world.

Many times Peter reaches back into history to compare past and present, even to showing that today news travels around the world at the speed of light. In computer science we no longer are in the days of sailing ships, million dollar CPUs and 128,000 US dollars for sixty-four kilobytes of core memory (which I paid in 1975). The world is changing rapidly, and the old proprietary models of developing software are dying.

The value of this book is to allow the reader to understand the past, to recognize the present and to be able to show people the future. I am proud that Peter asked me to write the foreword for his book.

Carpe Diem,
Jon "maddog" Hall

Introduction

This book is no history of computing, nor of the Internet. What follows won't be a predictable, chronological ordering of encysted events and petrified dates. Were you concerned about the absence of the first person singular pronoun in the above? Fear not.

Here I am. I am with you. And after my noisy disavowal of history, I must go back into it, back to the words of Sir Philip Sidney.

In his *Defence of Poesy* (1595), Sir Philip contrasts the historian, who is obliged to be faithful to recorded events, to the poet, who is capable of depicting ideals, employing imaginative fictions. To Sidney, the poet's superiority lies with clarity of moral vision, whereas the details of events may result in the blurring of the historian's vision.

Spenser (1552–1599), referring to himself as a "Poet historical," views historians as forced to follow orderly chronology, where poets can move back and forth in time. All of this is to attempt to excuse my moving ahead, and then swinging back, perhaps illustrating my drift between historian and "Poet historical." What I want to talk about is economics and computing, business and sociology, imagination and tradition.

This book will be about the way that computing and imagination are breaking the models of traditional business. About why the way that things have developed will bring about new ways of doing things, new businesses and new avenues for creativity. Karl Marx wrote that "All nations with a capitalist mode of production are seized periodically by a feverish attempt to make money without the mediation of the process of production." Tulip speculation in the Netherlands in the 1630s and the "dotCom bubble" of the 1990s are notable incidents in the history of this mania. Two centuries before Marx and one-and-a-half after.

About 60 years ago, Joseph Schumpeter (1883–1950) published *Capitalism, Socialism and Democracy* (1942; 2nd Ed., 1944; 3rd Ed., 1950) in which he coined the phrase "creative destruction."

Schumpeter felt that capitalism would not survive, not because it would be overthrown by a Marxist proletariat, but because it would be destroyed by its successes. He believed that capitalism would give rise to a large intellectual class that subsisted by attacking the bourgeois system of private property and freedom which were necessary for the class's existence. Schumpeter lauded the entrepreneur, who figures out how to use inventions, who introduces new means of production, and new forms of organization. It is innovation by the entrepreneur, he claimed, which leads to "creative destruction" as old inventories, ideas, technologies, skills become obsolete.

I believe that the increasing ubiquity of the Internet together with Free/Libre/Open Software is the force that drives today's "gales" of creative destruction. Well, we've all got cell phones, and TVs, and every candy bar has a URL on it. And nearly everything carries a bar code. But does that really change everything? Yes, it does.

Less than 200 years ago, each bolt came with its own individually fabricated nut. A lock came with a singular key. Blake's "dark satanic mills" had brought about some factories, but it was only the beginning of the industrial revolution. And that, itself, had been created by the new science that had developed in the two centuries before Blake.

From the end of the nineteenth century, scientific and engineering development has been seen to emanate from large labs: Edison, Kodak, Bell/AT&T, DuPont, BASF, Bayer, Lilly, Corning, Shell, IBM, etc., etc. But it was a widely distributed and unorganized band of scholars whose work led to the conceptual revolution that produced the modern world.

For example, Copernicus (1473–1543) observed the heavens and recorded his measurements. In 1563, Tycho Brahe (1546–1601) noted that Copernicus' figures weren't quite right, so, from 1577 to 1597, Tycho recorded extraordinarily accurate astronomical measurements. In 1599 Tycho moved from Denmark to Prague, where Johannes Kepler (1571–1630) was his assistant, until he succeeded him in 1601, when Tycho died. Before Copernicus, the universe was geocentric. This planet was the focus of all celestial bodies, as well as of God's attention.

Copernicus' work established heliocentricity. Tycho found that circular orbits just didn't work, and devoted decades to better measurements, which Kepler later used to determine that the orbits were ellipses, not circles. Tycho, incidentally, was glad that Copernicus' circles weren't right, for he was a geocentrist himself. (In 1610, Galileo [1564–1642] pointed out that one could observe phases on Venus, and that therefore Venus must be nearer the Sun than the Earth was.) And, Newton (1643–1727) showed us the force (gravity) that held everything in place. Poland. Denmark. Austria. Italy. Germany. England. Despite the religious strife, the 30 Years' War, turmoil in the Netherlands, in France, and in England, thought moved by means of print and in correspondence.

Though countries were at war and religions were in conflict, scientific exchange of ideas and sharing of data persisted. During the Renaissance it could take months for findings or observations to reach those interested in other countries. In the seventeenth and eighteenth centuries lengthy epistles between scholars were distributed to others beyond the addressees. Scientific journals followed. Thanks to the progress of communications media, it now takes seconds where it once took decades for an idea or a discovery to proliferate. The fact is undeniable: Invention and scholarship have been the motor driving the development of civilization and culture. The revolution of knowledge led us to exploration and discovery.

The computer, the Internet, and the Web have led to a similar revolution. While certainly no computer user, Thomas Jefferson, in a letter to Isaac McPherson (13 August 1813), wrote:

> *If nature has made any one thing less susceptible than all others of exclusive property, it is the action of the thinking power called an idea, which an individual may exclusively possess as long as he keeps it to himself; but the moment it is divulged, it forces itself into the possession of every one, and the receiver cannot dispossess himself of it.*

The advent of the computer and the Internet have given rise to the expansion of the academic/scholarly notions of sharing, and this in turn has brought us free and open software, which will bring about major change in the ways we do business. Change yields opportunity. But change also requires adaptability. We are embarking on a new business model, which will change the way we do business as much as mass production and global electronic communication did over the 19th and 20th centuries.

Over four centuries have passed since our static geocentric universe was replaced by a dynamic one. Today, the business model that has persisted since the late eighteenth century is being replaced. Colonialism, imperialism, capitalism are all founded in hierarchic authoritarianism. Free/open/libre source embodies something else: not really socialism or communism. Perhaps cooperativism?

1 The Opaque Crystal Ball

Despite the fact that fools predict the future all the time — betting on horse races, buying lottery tickets, consulting the *Farmer's Almanac* — we're all pretty bad at it. My guess is that only seers (and seeresses) and bookies make money from the predictions. And, of course, political and economic pundits (seers in bad suits). (I've often wondered why people purchase methods to make a fortune playing poker, betting on horses, or "beating" the stock market. Surely, were the vendors of such methods successful, they themselves would be multi-millionaires. But their earnings seem to originate from the gullible. By the way, are you interested in a bridge? ...)

We don't do very well on a technological level, either. Alexander Graham Bell was sure that no one would ever want a telephone in their home. Lord Kelvin predicted that radio had no future (and that heavier than air flight was impossible). Thomas Watson was advised that the world demand for computers was five. Ken Olsen (the founder of DEC) was sure no one would want a computer in their home. And only 35 years ago, it was predicted that the ARPANET (the parent of the Internet) might grow to as many as 2000 users. There is a (mythical?) Chinese proverb: "To prophesy is extremely difficult — especially with regard to the future."

Let's look at a few events of the late 1960s.

- In June 1968, the Federal Communications Commission's "Carterphone" decision compelled AT&T to allow its customers to connect non-Western Electric equipment to the telephone network. (FCC Docket Number 16942; 13 FCC 2nd, 420.)

- In July 1968, Andrew Grove and Gordon Moore founded Intel.

  In August 1968, William G. McGowan established Microwave Communications of America (MCI) and the FCC ruled that MCI could compete with AT&T, using microwave transport between Chicago and St. Louis.

- In December 1968, the Defense Advanced Research Projects Agency let a contract to Bolt, Beranek and Newman of Cambridge, Mass., for just over $1 million. The contract was for a packet-switching network of four nodes.

Four more events followed the next year.

- In July, humans landed on the moon.

- August saw the invention of UNIX.

- In the autumn, the first four nodes of the ARPANET went up.

- And, in December, Linus Torvalds was born. (Who? Read on ...)

Had anyone asked, I would have thought the first of these events was the most important. NASA (with modesty) says: "On July 20, 1969, the human race accomplished its single greatest technological achievement of all time when a human first set foot on another celestial body."

As of the outset of the Twenty-First century, NASA had brought us "Tang" but has taken us nowhere. The other items in this list have proven to be the stuff of revolution.

2 Ancient History

Aids to calculation, like the abacus, are quite old; and mechanical calculation dates from the seventeenth century, but mechanical computation is far more recent. Though first conceived by Charles Babbage in 1823, the computer as we know it needed more than a century to come into being.

The first true electro-mechanical (part mechanical, part electrical) computer was Harold Aiken's Mark I (conceived in 1937 and put into operation at Harvard in 1944) and the first fully electronic machine was Maurice Wilkes' EDSAC (1949) in the UK. Folks argue about these, wanting to give the credit to Atanasoff (Iowa) or Konrad Zuse (Germany, then Switzerland) or Turing (UK). I'll stick to Aiken and Wilkes.

You can get into arguments about "commercial" computers, too. There was the LEO (Lyons' Electronic Office — that's right, special bookkeeping machines built for a chain of tea shops) in the UK — but it never did fulfill its promise. There were freight-car-sized constructs by Burroughs and Remington Rand and ... But the winner was really IBM.

What I'd call the first commercial computer, the IBM 701, wasn't completed until late in 1952. The first production machine was shipped from Poughkeepsie, N.Y., to the IBM headquarters building in Manhattan that December. The second machine was destined for Los Alamos, N.Mex., and production continued in IBM's Poughkeepsie facility through June 1954, when machine 18 was shipped to Burbank, Calif. That's a rather slow rate of production by our standards, but literally everything was new in the early 1950s.[1]

---

[1] By 1954, IBM realized that there had to be a better way to do programming,

3

Prior to the 701, all computers had been one-offs. Aiken's, Wilkes', ENIAC (in Princeton, N.J.), etc.; each was *sui generis*. The 701 was a genuine breakthrough. On 7 May 1954, the redesigned 701 was announced as the IBM 704. It was more than merely a redesign. The 704 was incompatible with the 701. (Sounds just like successive versions of Microsoft. The industry still hasn't learned about backward compatibility.) The 704 had 4096 words of magnetic core memory. It had three index registers. It employed the full, 36-bit word (as opposed to the 701's 18-bit words). It had floating-point arithmetic. It could perform 40,000 instructions per second. While deliveries began in late 1955, the operators (today we would think of them as system administrators) of the eighteen 701s were already fretful. (Actually, there were nineteen 701s, the first having gone to IBM World Headquarters.)

Eventually (by 1960), 123 IBM 704 systems were sold. IBM itself had no solution to the problem of educating the operators. Though IBM had hosted a "training class" for customers of the 701 in August 1952, there were no courses, no textbooks. (After all, they just built stuff and sold it: Who would have imagined that purchasers would need training, that they might have problems? And no one had ever heard of an 800-number or a "Help Desk.") But several of the participants in the training class decided to continue to meet informally and discuss mutual problems. (According to E.W. Pugh, their first meeting was "in February 1953 during an AIEE-IRE Computer Conference in Los Angeles.")

The participants agreed to hold a second meeting after their own 701s had been installed. That meeting was hosted by Douglas Aircraft in Santa Monica in August 1953. There were other informal meetings and then, following an IBM Symposium, The RAND Corporation hosted a meeting in Los Angeles in August 1955 of representatives from all seventeen organizations that

---

and set up a multi-institute group to create a "Formula-Translation" language (FORTRAN). The first FORTRAN manual was produced on 12 October 1956.

had ordered 704s. It was at this meeting that the world's first computer user group was formed: It was called SHARE.

IBM encouraged the operators to meet, to discuss their problems, and to share their solutions to those problems. IBM funded the meetings as well as making a library of 300 computer programs available to members. SHARE, 50 years later, is still the place where IBM customers gain information. (A number of the earliest contributed programs are still available.) The importance of SHARE can be seen in the fact that in December 1955, early purchasers of Remington Rand's ERA1103A emulated their colleagues, forming an organization called USE (Univac Scientific Exchange). In 1956, user groups for Burroughs and Bendix computers were formed, as well as IBM's GUIDE, for users of their business computers.

Though SHARE was vendor-sponsored at the outset, today it is an independent organization.

User groups are one thread in the complex fabric from which this book was cut.

Another is communication.

DARPA and IPTO

In response to the USSR's launching of Sputnik in October 1957, the US Department of Defense established the Defense Advanced Research Projects Agency (DARPA — The basic "charge" of the Agency has not changed significantly.). That charge was "to think independently of the rest of the military and to respond quickly and innovatively to national defense challenges."[2]

In 1962, Jack Ruina, the Director of DARPA, hired J. C. R.

---

[2]DoD directive 5105.15 (7 February 1958) set up "The Advanced Research Projects Agency" (ARPA). On 23 March 1972, by DoD directive, the name was changed to DARPA. On 22 February 1993, DARPA was "redesignated" ARPA, and on 22 February 1996, Public Law 104-106 (Title IX of the FY 1996 Defense Authorization Act) directed an "organizational name change" to DARPA.

Licklider to be the first Director of DARPA's new Information Processing Techniques Office (IPTO). Licklider (1915–1990) has been called the Father of Artificial Intelligence, the Father of Cybernetics, the Father of the ARPANET, and of many other things. He was brilliant and foresighted. Originally, the IPTO was to extend research into the computerization of the air defense system. The IPTO funded research into advanced computer (and networking) technologies and funded fifteen groups to do research in human-computer interaction and distributed systems.[3]

In 1963, Lick (as many called him) funded Project MAC at MIT, which was headed by Robert Fano.[4] Just what MAC stood for is unclear: some claim it was Machine-Aided-Cognition, some that it was Multiple-Access Computers. On the fifth floor of Tech Square in Cambridge, Mass., it was the latter. On the ninth floor (where Marvin Minsky's artificial intelligence lab was located) it was known as Man-and-Computer.

Project MAC explored the potential for communities on time-sharing machines. That is, relationships among the uses and the users of shared mainframes. And this leads directly to the next strand in our narrative: time-sharing.

Time-Sharing

John McCarthy had begun thinking about time-sharing in the mid-1950s. But it was only at MIT in 1961–62 that he, Jack Dennis and Fernando Corbato talked seriously about permitting "each

---

[3] Among the research sites were: Carnegie-Mellon University, MIT, the RAND Corporation, the Stanford Research Institute, the System Development Corporation, UC Berkeley, UC Santa Barbara, UCLA, the University of Southern California, and the University of Utah.

[4] Fano (1917–) was born in Turin, Italy, and studied there until he emigrated to the US in 1939. He received his Sc.D. from MIT and joined its faculty in 1947. He has done important work in information theory (with "the father of information theory" Claude Elwood Shannon), microwave transmission and networking.

user of a computer to behave as though he were in sole control of a computer."[5]

When McCarthy went to MIT from Dartmouth in 1957, it was clear that time-sharing the IBM 704 would require an interrupt system which didn't exist yet. So McCarthy proposed a hardware solution involving a relay whereby the 704 could be set to "trapping mode" by an external signal. But, like many other brilliant insights, McCarthy's notion went undeveloped for several years.

Four years later, MIT had a transistorized computer, the IBM 7090, and so Corbato wrote CTSS (Compatible Time-Sharing System). While it had bugs, it was a wild success, influencing systems at Dartmouth (DTSS) and the Incompatible Time-Sharing System (ITS) for the PDP-10s at MIT (note that over 40 years ago, geeks were already making geek jokes. More about this later[6]). At the same time, Licklider noted just how many different multimillion dollar computers he was funding, each of which was a solitude, unable to communicate with others.

In early 1963 he sent a memo to "Members and Affiliates of the Intergalactic Computer Network" — the principal investigators at the sites he had endowed. He consistently asserted that the computer was a communications, not a computation device. Then he returned to MIT.

Lick's successor at the IPTO was Robert Taylor. He was interested in networking and, in 1966, was funding 17 sites with a variety of incompatibilities. He needed help; and he found it in Larry Roberts. Roberts had been working at the Lincoln Laboratory in Massachusetts since 1963. While there, he and Thomas Marill had conducted a networking experiment con-

---

[5]McCarthy received his Ph.D. from Princeton in 1951 and coined the term "Artificial Intelligence" at the 1955 Dartmouth Conference. He was the creator of Lisp and received the 1971 Turing Award.

[6]Project MAC was also the place where "daemon" was coined as the name for a process running in the background of the IBM 7094. Corbato says it was based on James Clerk Maxwell's thought experiment involving what we call "Maxwell's daemon" in thermodynamics.

necting the Systems Development Corporation's AN/FSQ-32 in Santa Monica, Calif., with the TX-2 at Lincoln via a 1200 bits per second dedicated phone link. This permitted any program on one machine to dial the other computer, log in and run a program from a server (somewhat like a subroutine call).[7]

Roberts and Marill presented their results at the AFIPS Fall Joint Conference in 1966. While this was quite an achievement, it really did not further the aim of ARPA, except to demonstrate that long-distance data transfer via telephone wires was indeed feasible. That remote calculation was possible over phone lines had already been demonstrated by George Stibitz[8] in 1940, from a Teletype at Dartmouth in New Hampshire to his calculator at Bell Labs. (The young Norbert Weiner spent two days trying the "stump" the calculator.)

And it was now a quarter-century since then. Ivan Sutherland and Bob Taylor wanted Roberts to come to Washington to work on the networking technology. Larry didn't want to go. So Taylor went to Charlie Herzfeld (who was the head of ARPA at that time). "Look, you fund 51% of Lincoln Lab," Bob said, "why don't you call them up and tell them to send Larry down here?" Herzfeld called. And the director of Lincoln Lab told Roberts: "I think that you really ought to go to ARPA." So Roberts did "within a week or two." Herzfeld remarked to me at the 25th Anniversary festivity, "It was only mild blackmail."

At ARPA, Larry suggested building the IPTO network on the basis of the work he and Marill had already done. Roberts had a lot of enthusiasm and foresight: it was he who stated that networking would foster "a 'community' use of computers." In

---

[7]The TX-2 had been installed at Lincoln Lab in 1958, the successor to the TX-0 (1955), the first transistorized computer. The original team included Wesley Clark as the designer and Ken Olsen — who would soon go off to found DEC — as the engineer-in-charge. The TX-2 was the computer on which Ivan Sutherland in 1959 designed and ran Sketchpad, the first graphics program. SDC's AN/FSQ-32 ran TSS (Time-Sharing System) in 1963, which had been designed in response to a challenge from Licklider.
[8]1904–1995

April 1967, Roberts and Taylor took advantage of the meeting of the IPTO Principal Investigators at the University of Michigan in Ann Arbor to talk up their ideas of a network. Some of the PIs were interested in "resource sharing," but the contractors in attendance set up a sub-group, "Communication Group," to work on problems. Among those problems were the conventions to be used in communications and the kinds of communications lines. It was agreed that work should be begun on the conventions and that the connections would be via dial-up lines.

The plan as developed was for the computer sites to be connected via commercial phone lines and data sets (modems), so that each computer could be connected with every other computer via circuit-switching. During the discussion, Wesley Clark (who had moved to Washington University in St. Louis from Lincoln Lab) had an idea. He thought about it and described it to Roberts after the meeting during a shared cab ride (it was raining very hard) between Ann Arbor and the Detroit airport.

Clark's notion was that the problems of working out the many possible connections could be solved by placing a mini-computer on each site. These [identical] mini-computers would communicate with each other and each site would only have to concern itself with the task of communicating with its mini. Roberts incorporated the idea into his summary of the meeting, "Message Switching Network Proposal," which he sent out on April 27, 1967. He called the mini an "Interface Message Processor." The IMP was born.

Clark was extremely modest about this. "Someone else would have thought of it in a few days or weeks," he remarked to me.

But his notion was both insightful and influential. Putting the IMPS — minicomputers — into the network design made it easier for the designers to specify most of the network: they no longer had to worry about the various host computers. Nearly a year later, on March 1, 1968, the IPTO reported to the Director of ARPA that the specifications were "essentially complete." Larry

Roberts submitted a "program plan" to the Director on June 3rd and it was approved on June 21st.

The ARPA budget for 1968 earmarked $500,000 for the ARPANET. ARPA sent out a Request for Quotation to 140 potential bidders. The Defense Supply Service — Washington received twelve proposals. Four of the bidders were deemed to be in contention and, finally, the week before Christmas 1968, the contract was awarded to BBN (Bolt, Beranek & Newman) in Cambridge, Massachusetts. Work at BBN began on January 2, 1969. Discussions and planning began early in the year at the four institutions. By the end of December, there were four nodes on the ARPANET: UCLA, SRI, UCSB, and the University of Utah.[9]

---

[9]For a far more detailed story of the development of the Internet, see my *Casting the Net* (1995).

Excursus: Law

In 1949, the Truman Department of Justice filed suit against AT&T and Western Electric, claiming the companies were acting "in restraint of trade."

On 24 January 1956, Judge Thomas F. Meaney entered a "consent decree," in which the companies were enjoined "from commencing ... manufacture for sale or lease any equipment" other than that used in providing telephone or telegraph services; from "engaging ... in any business not of a character or type engaged in by Western or its subsidiaries ... "; and AT&T was enjoined "from engaging ... in any business other than the furnishing of common carrier communications services."

There were a few exceptions. Exception (b) was "experiments for the purpose of testing or developing new common carrier communications services." AT&T was further required to reveal the patents it held and to license these when asked.

No one could have foreseen the problems that this consent decree would entail.

The Daemon, the Gnu, and the Penguin

3 UNIX

In spring 1969, AT&T decided to terminate its involvement in a project called Multics — Multiplexed Information and Computing Service — which had been started in 1964 by MIT, GE and Bell Labs. This left those at AT&T's Bell Labs who had been working on the project, notably Doug McIlroy, Dennis Ritchie and Ken Thompson, at loose ends. Doug immediately got involved with other things in Murray Hill, N.J., but Dennis and Ken had been interested in the project *per se* and wanted to explore several of its ideas.

Ken has said:

> Dennis and [Rudd] Canaday and I were discussing these ideas of the general nature of keeping the files out of each other's hair and the nitty-gritty of expanding, of the real implementation where you put block addresses ... We did it in Canaday's office, and, at the end of the discussion, Canaday picked up the phone; there was a new service at Bell Laboratories that took dictation. You call up essentially a tape recorder and you give notes, and then the next morning the notes are typed and sent to you. The next day these notes came back, and all the acronyms were butchered, like 'inode' was 'eyen...'. So we got back these descriptions and they were copied, and we each had copies of them and they became the working document for the file system — which was just built in a day or two on the PDP-7.
>
> At first ... we used it for other things, you know, the

13

famous Space Travel game, and it was the natural candidate as the place to put the file system. When we hacked out this design, this rough design of the file system on the dictation [machine] that day in Canaday's office, I went off and implemented it on the PDP-7.

I won't go into full detail on the evolution of that file system on the PDP-7 to Unics (Uniplexed Information and Computing Service, a pun on cut-down [emasculated] Multics devised by Peter Neumann[1], an inveterate punster. Several people told me that Brian Kernighan had changed the spelling to UNIX, but Brian told me that he had not, and that no one recalled who had done it). For now, it is important to realize that the system was the cooperative product of several brilliant minds: Ritchie, Thompson and Canaday, of whom Robert Morris, Sr. (who joined Bell Labs in 1960 and retired from the National Computer Security Center in Maryland) said he was the "most underrated" of the original participants[2], as well as other "contributors," like Doug McIlroy.

In August 1969. Ken Thompson's wife Bonnie took their year-old son on a trip to California to show him off to their families. As a temporary bachelor, Ken had time to work.

I allocated a week each to the operating system, the shell, the editor and the assembler [he told me] ... and during the month she was gone, it was totally rewritten in a form that looked like an operating system, with tools that were sort of known, you know,

---

[1]Peter G. Neumann holds doctorates from Harvard and Darmstadt. After a decade at Bell Labs, he moved to SRI in 1971 and has remained there. Among other things, Neumann is the co-founder of People for Internet Responsibility and chairs the National Committee for Voting Integrity.

[2]Canaday graduated from Harvard in 1959 and subsequently received M.S. and Ph.D. Degrees from MIT. He spent 25 years at Bell Labs, taking early retirement in 1989. Canaday was the manager of the Programmer's Workbench "gang."

assembler, editor, and shell — if not maintaining itself, right on the verge of maintaining itself, to totally
sever the GECOS connection .... Yeh, essentially one
person for a month.

It didn't exist by itself for very long ... maybe a day
or two before we started developing the things we
needed.

While Multics certainly influenced UNIX, there were
also profound differences.

Dennis Ritchie explained:

We were a bit oppressed by the big system mentality.
Ken wanted to do something simple. Presumably, as
important as anything was the simple fact that our
means were much smaller — we could get only small
machines with none of the fancy Multics hardware.

So UNIX wasn't quite a reaction against Multics, it
was more a combination of these things. Multics
wasn't there for us any more, but we liked the feel
of interactive computing that it offered; Ken had
some ideas about how to do a system that he had
to work out; and the hardware available as well as
our inclinations tended to trying to build neat small
things, instead of grandiose ones.

Thompson "scarfed up" a PDP-7 and "did this neat stuff with
it," Ritchie told me, modestly. Thompson created a new toy that
would initiate work on a new system all over the world.

Soon a PDP-11 was acquired and UNIX was rewritten and ex-
panded and rewritten. With McIlroy prodding, Dennis and Ken
produced a "UNIX Programmer's Manual" (dated "November 3,
1971). A "Second Edition" was issued June 12, 1972: "the number
of UNIX installations has grown to 10, with more expected," the
Preface told us. Third Edition of the manual appeared "February,

1973," and noted that there were "now" 16 installations. That was soon to wax quite rapidly.

All of the first 10 installations were at AT&T in New Jersey. In the late summer of 1972, UNIX leaped across the Hudson River to an office on the 14th floor of 330 Madison Avenue in Manhattan. Neil Groundwater had joined New York Telephone upon graduating from Penn State. He commuted from his apartment in Manhattan to Whippany, N.J., where he worked on programming for the Electronic Switching System. But being in Whippany placed him in proximity to Bell Labs and he began learning about UNIX. It was no easy task. "There was documentation on some parts," he told me. "But as we would come to say years later, 'Use the source, Luke'" was the sole answer to many questions.[3]

In October 1973, Dennis Ritchie and Ken Thompson drove up the Hudson Valley to the new IBM Research Center at Yorktown Heights to deliver the first UNIX paper at the Symposium on Operating System Principles (SOSP).

"It was a beautiful fall day," Dennis remarked. Ken, who delivered the paper, told me: "The audience was several hundred. I was pretty nervous. The response was the normal, polite applause. I don't recall any questions."

Ken was over-modest. The audience was quite enthusiastic. Ken and Dennis were immediately asked for copies of the new system.

This put the AT&T lawyers in a bind: was a computer operating system part of "common carrier communications services"? Was AT&T required to distribute UNIX?

The decision of the corporate lawyers was that Bell Labs should distribute UNIX to academic and research institutions at the cost of the media involved plus a shipping charge. Within a few months, several dozen institutions requested UNIX.

---

[3]The detailed history of the development of UNIX can be found in my *A Quarter Century of UNIX* (Addison-Wesley, 1994). Groundwater's narrative is in Chapter 7.

4 The Users

Let's go back to the mid-1950s. At the time that Judge Meaney was considering the action against AT&T, IBM was coming out with the 704, the upgrade of the 701. As mentioned earlier, the transitioning from the 701 to the 704 wasn't easy, so some of the IBM "operators" formed the organization still known as SHARE.

Almost immediately, many computer manufacturers were sponsoring user organizations. DECUS — the DEC Users' Society — first met in 1961. It soon had a British branch (DECUS UK), and rapidly became yet more international. In but a few years, Prime and Apollo had user organizations as well — PRIMUS and ADUS.

So, by the beginning of 1974 there were a number of user groups exchanging information and a new operating system that was beginning to get folks excited. No one had thought seriously about licensing. And there were 40 nodes on the ARPANET.

Early in 1974, Mel Ferentz (then at Brooklyn College)[1] and Lou Katz[2] (then at Columbia's College of Physicians and Surgeons) called a meeting of UNIX users in New York in May. Ken Thompson supplied them with a list of those who had requested a copy of UNIX after the SOSP meeting. Nearly three dozen had done so in under six months ... and all had either been at the meeting or had heard about it by word of mouth.

The meeting took place on May 15, 1974. The agenda was a simple one: descriptions of several installations and uses;

---

[1] Mel went on to Rockefeller University and later became one of the founders of NYSERNET; Lou moved to UC Berkeley in 1981. He was the founding President of the USENIX Association.

[2] Lou was the first recipient of a 9-track tape of UNIX from Ken at Bell Labs.

lunch; "Ken Thompson speaks!"; interchange of UNIX hints; interchange of DEC hints; free-for-all discussion. Lou told me that he thought there were about 20 people in attendance; Mel thought it might have been a few more than that. That's the organization that's now USENIX.[3]

The Ritchie-Thompson paper appeared in the July 1974 issue of *Communications of the ACM*. The editor described it as "elegant." Soon, Ken was awash in requests for UNIX.

Mike O'Dell's reaction to the article is typical. In 1974, Mike was an undergraduate at the University of Oklahoma. He told me:

> We had this thing called ITF — the Intermittent Terminal Facility – which had the world's worst implementation of BASIC, and one of the guys had written some routines which let you do I/O on terminals — and this was a non-trivial feat. So a group of us sat down and tried to figure out whether we could do something interesting . . . .
>
> The UNIX issue came. I remember going down the hall and getting it out of my mailbox and saying to myself, Oh, ACM's got something on operating systems, maybe it's worth reading. And I started reading through it. I remember reading this paper on the UNIX time-sharing system. It was sort of like being hit in the head with a rock. And I reread it. And I got up and went out of my office, around the corner to George Maybry who was one of the other guys involved with this. And I threw the issue down on his desk and said: "How could this many people have been so wrong for so long?"
>
> And he said: "What are you talking about?"

---

[3] Again, see *A Quarter-Century of UNIX* for details.

And I said: "Read this and then try to tell me that what we've been doing is not just nuts. We've been crazy. This is what we want."

The *CACM* article most definitely had a dramatic impact. Today, things would be quite different. Lou Katz wouldn't have relied on written notices; Ferentz might not have produced a purple-Dittoed newsletter. O'Dell wouldn't have gleaned the news from *CACM*, but from email and the Internet and the Web..

By 1975, the ARPANET (with 60 nodes and soon to turn into the Internet) was becoming a way of distributing information. In 1969, what we would think of as telnet and ftp were all there was. Then, in 1970, Ray Tomlinson invented email (which soon became the principal use of the ARPANET), and in May 1975, RFC 681, "Network UNIX," appeared.[4] Written by Steve Holmgren, Steve Bunch and Gary Grossman, the RFC began:

INTRODUCTION

THE UNIX TIME-SHARING SYSTEM PRESENTS SEVERAL INTERESTING CAPABILITIES AS AN ARPA NETWORK MINI-HOST. IT OFFERS POWERFUL LOCAL PROCESSING FACILITIES IN TERMS OF USER PROGRAMS, SEVERAL COMPILERS, AN EDITOR BASED ON QED, A VERSATILE DOCUMENT PREPARATION SYSTEM, AND AN EFFICIENT FILE SYSTEM FEATURING SOPHISTICATED ACCESS CONTROL, MOUNTABLE AND DE-MOUNTABLE VOLUMES, AND A UNIFIED TREATMENT OF PERIPHERALS AS SPECIAL FILES.

The secret, such as it was, was out. Several people expressed their strong feelings as to just how this "put UNIX on the Net." I feel that the effect was more powerful: over the next few years, the result was that the Internet was run on UNIX. The protocols

---

[4]The RFCs are "Requests for Comment," the net's consensual standards.

The Daemon, the Gnu, and the Penguin

were all in tune with the "UNIX Philosophy." What we would now call "source" was widely available. Anyone actually running UNIX had accessible source. This meant that there could be true communication and we were approaching interoperability. The direct result was that UNIX was soon in use throughout the world: Japan and Australia; most of Europe; North America.

Just how widespread UNIX was is illustrated in Ferentz' first mailing list (July 30, 1975) published in *UNIX NEWS*:

The First Mailing List

Bell Telephone Labs	Brooklyn College
Carleton College	Case Western Reserve Univ.
The Children's Museum	City University of New York
Columbia University	Duke Medical Center
East Brunswick High School	Harvard University
Hebrew University of Jerusalem	Heriot-Watt University
Johns Hopkins University	Knox College
Naval Postgraduate School	Oregon Museum of Science
Polytechnic University of N.Y.	Princeton University
The Rand Corporation	St. Olaf College
Stanford University	The Spence School
Univ. Catholique de Louvain	University of Alberta
U. of California, Berkeley	U. of Manitoba
U. of North Carolina	U. of Saskatchewan
U. of Texas at Dallas	U. of Toronto
U. of Utah	U. of Waterloo
U. of Wisconsin	

The US, Scotland, Belgium, and Canada; universities and museums; a public high school and a private girls' school. In one year from publication. But in mid-1975, few of these establishments had electronic connectivity. In a few years, that would change and many (if not all) of the user sites would have some sort of network connection.

Another problem was hardware. In 1975, if you wanted to run UNIX, you needed a PDP-11 from DEC. That, too, was to change.

The change came about first at Princeton and then, simultaneously, at two sites about half the world apart from one another: Bell Labs in Murray Hill, N.J., and the Wollongong satellite campus of the University of New South Wales in Australia.[5]

First, at Princeton, in 1976 and 1977, Tom Lyon enabled some parts of UNIX to run under VM/360 on an IBM 360. It was only the first step.

At the Labs, in 1977–78, Dennis Ritchie and Steve Johnson ported UNIX to the Interdata 8/32; in Australia, Richard Miller and his colleagues were porting UNIX to the Interdata 7/32.[6] Dennis Ritchie has said that porting to the Interdata was both a challenge and the achievement he was most proud of, for it demonstrated that UNIX could be ported to non-DEC hardware. Steve Johnson told me that once one had ported something to an alien architecture, one knew better than to ever try it again. He referred to the Interdata as the "Intersnail."

But Australia? Yes.

John Lions read the *CACM* article in the summer of 1974, when the University of New South Wales was about to get a PDP-11/40, and the University negotiated a license with Western Electric.[7] In 1975–76, UNIX was a real hit on the UNSW campus. But Lions had a problem. He wanted to use UNIX in teaching operating systems. But there was no textbook and there was no explicated version of the code — v6 (Version 6 or 6th Edition). So Lions decided to do something about the lack: he wrote a commentary on the code (9073 lines at that time) and received permission from Western Electric to print out the code and commentary for instructional purposes. UNSW duplicated

---

[5]The University of Wollongong is now independent.

[6]Interdata, later bought by Perkin-Elmer, brought out the 7/32 in 1974 and the 8/32 the following year.

[7]See Chapter 15 of *A Quarter-Century of UNIX*.

the code in red cardboard covers and the commentary in orange. They were as big a hit as the system.

The March 1977 issue of *UNIX NEWS* (vol. 2, no. 3) announced the availability of the books (to licensees) together with a note by Mel Ferentz: "Ken Thompson has seen the first version of the book and reports that it is a good job" (I think that's quite a review.) The price, including airmail, was $A17.70 (under $20 US, at that time). The *UKUUG Newsletter* announced the availability of the code and commentary, too, but the next issue said that future orders should be placed with Bell Laboratories and by late 1978 the volumes were no longer available. (The Labs' reproductions were in a single volume bound in black.)

Someone at AT&T/Western Electric had woken up. Freely available documentation wasn't a good thing.

But, once again, the proverbial cat was out of the bag.

Over the years, over nearly two decades, John Lions' "Code and Commentary" became the most copied work in computing. The volumes carry the appropriate copyright notices and the restriction to licensees, but there was no way that Western Electric could stem their circulation. They were just too valuable. (I admit that I possess an nth-generation photocopy as well as treasured copies, in orange and red covers, inscribed to me by John Lions.)[8]

Why care? Because here we were in the mid-1970s with the users taking control and determining what to distribute where information was concerned. Luckily, Western Electric was no more successful at controlling that information than Popes Paul V and Urban VIII were when Galileo wrote of heliocentricity. But note again: In the 1970s, you received Lions' work in hard copy, via airmail. Thirty years ago there wasn't the availability of electronic access we have today.

Similarly, the inability of the AT&T/Western Electric lawyers

---

[8]In 1996, after a great deal of correspondence and with the active assistance of Dennis Ritchie, I succeeded in getting permission from both AT&T and The Santa Cruz Operation to reprint Lions' work. ISBN 1-57398-013-1.

to decide just what was permissible led an announcement in *UNIX NEWS* (30 April 1976) that Lew Law of the Harvard Science Center was:

> ... willing to undertake the task of reproducing and distributing the manuals for UNIX .... 'The UNIX PROGRAMMER'S MANUAL' Sixth Edition dated May 1975 will be reproduced in its entirety. Most installations will want to remove several pages ...

The May-June 1976 issue announced "the first mailing from the Software Exchange." This first software tape contained Harvard software; the duplication and mailing was done by Mike O'Brien, then at the University of Illinois at Chicago Circle. Mike told me that the idea had come to him at an early UNIX Users' meeting. "I'm just greedy," he said. "I had to get the newest software as soon as possible. I had to be the first. And this was a way to get the latest and neatest as soon as possible. So I suggested it to Mel. It wasn't altruism at all"

The second software tape was announced in November 1976, along with the following note from O'Brien:

> I got the "diff" listing of all changes to Bell UNIX system proper from "standard" version 6 ... Anyway, I've itemized some 50 changes, and sent the list to Ken for verification and comments. The changes will be available through the center by special request.

That second distribution tape contained contributions from the RAND Corporation, the Naval Postgraduate School, the University of California at San Diego, Yale, and UIUC. The Third Software Distribution was announced in May 1977. The last USENIX distribution was in 1988 and consisted of two 10-inch reels.

The 50-bugs tape (O'Brien's 50 changes) has an interesting tale connected to it.

Ken Thompson told me:

The first thing to realize is that the outside world ran on releases of UNIX (V4, V5, V6, V7) but we did not. Our view was a continuum.

After V6, I was preparing to go to Berkeley to teach for a year. I was putting together a system to take. Since it was almost a release, I made a "diff" with V6. On the way to Berkeley, I stopped by Urbana-Champaign to keep an eye on Greg Chesson[9] who was finishing up his Ph.D. (subtle recruiting). I left the "diff" tape there and told him that I wouldn't mind it if it got around. (I think I gave it to others too, perhaps Katz.) ...

Lou Katz' version is a bit different:

A large number of bug fixes was collected, and rather than issue them one at a time, a collection tape was put together by Ken. Some of the fixes were quite important ... I suspect that a significant number of the fixes were actually done by non-Bell people. Ken tried to send it out, but the lawyers kept stalling and stalling and stalling.

Finally, someone "found" a tape on Mountain Avenue (The address of Bell Laboratories was 600 Mountain Avenue, Murray Hill, N.J.) which had the fixes.

When the lawyers found out about it, they called every licensee and threatened them with dire consequences if they didn't destroy the tape ... after trying to find out how they got the tape. I would guess that no one would actually tell them how they came by the tape (I didn't). It was the first of many attempts

---

[9]Chesson brought UNIX to the University of Illinois, where he received a Ph.D. in 1977. He went on to become one of the founders of Silicon Graphics.

by the AT&T lawyers to justify their existence and to kill UNIX.[10]

At this time AT&T had a strict policy of

- no advertising

- no support

- no bug fixes

- payment in advance

Twenty years earlier, IBM had seen that encouraging the users to cooperate and exchange was a benefit. AT&T still forced the users to band together and compelled them to share what they had learned and what they knew.

---

[10] At the 1994 USENIX technical meeting in Boston, there was a 25th birthday session after which Lou "confessed" that he had received a phone message at Columbia to the effect that if he drove down to Mountain Avenue "around 2pm," he'd "find" something of interest. So he and Reidar Bornholdt drove from Manhattan to Murray Hill and "found" the can with the tape in it. Ken told me that he had "no idea" how the tape could have gotten there. Dennis suggested that it might have "fallen from a truck." Everyone laughed. O'Brien later told me (at the 2005 USENIX Technical Conference in Anaheim) that he had "picked up" the fixes from the image Ken had "inadvertently" left on the machine when he visited Chesson at UIUC.

The Daemon, the Gnu, and the Penguin

5 A Tale of Two Editors

Interestingly, Bill Joy created vi in 1976 and Richard Stallman (together with Guy Steele and Dave Moon) created Emacs the same year.[1]

The original version of Emacs was based on TECMAC and TMACS, two TECO (Text Editor and COrrector) editors. Stallman and Michael McMahon ported it to the Tenex (for the DEC-10) and TOPS-20 (for the DEC-20) operating systems. (James Gosling, the creator of Oak/Java, wrote the first Emacs for UNIX at Carnegie-Mellon in 1981. Stallman began work on GNU EMACS in 1984.)

Joy's creation had a more varied origin.

The editor created by Ken Thompson in August 1969 was called ed. Ken had written a version of QED for CTSS on the IBM 7094 at MIT. He and Ritchie then wrote a version for the GE-635 (the "Multics machine") at Bell Labs. The cut-down version of this for the PDP-7 was ed. While TECO was known for its complex syntax, ed must have been (and still is) the most user-hostile editor ever created.

Across the Atlantic in London, George Coulouris at Queen Mary College (now Queen Mary and Wakefield College) had gotten UNIX v4 in late 1973. George explained to me how unhappy he had been with ed and how he created em (*editor for mortals*) so that QMC students could "exploit more effectively some vdu [visual display unit] that we had recently acquired ..."

---

[1] The detailed history of on-line text editors is quite complex, and will not be gone into.

The Daemon, the Gnu, and the Penguin

Then I spent the summer of 1976 as a visitor to the
CS Department at Berkeley. I worked in a room full
of teletype terminals using the departmental UNIX.
I had brought em with me on DECtape and installed
it there for my own use . . .

One day, sitting at the next terminal was this fairly
frenzied hacker/Ph.D. Student [Bill Joy] who told
me he was writing a Pascal compiler. I showed him
em, and he said "that's nice, the systems support
people might be interested in that." He took me and
introduced me to them. They had a couple of PDP-
11s . . . supporting several rooms full of vdu terminals
connected at 9600 baud, an environment in which
em could really shine.

I explained the em was an extension of ed that gave
key-stroke level interaction for editing within a single line, displaying the up-to-date line on the screen
(a sort of single-line screen editor) . . . The system support person [Jeff Schriebman] said something like:
"That's very nice, but if we made it available to all of
our users the overheads associated with running in
raw mode would swamp the cpu."

I was rather depressed by this reaction, thinking "I
guess I have been unrealistic in developing an editor
that is so expensive to run . . . "

Nevertheless, Bill and the support people took a copy
of my source to see if they would use it. I then went
to the East Coast for a week or so. When I returned,
I found that Bill had taken my code as a starting
point and had got a long way towards what was to
become ex and subsequently vi, and that the editor
was installed on the service machines . . .

1976! Created in 1969, ed had travelled west to Australia and
east to Vienna. Coulouris had created em in London and brought

it to Berkeley. Now the Berkeley editor, ex, would be available on the first UCB tape. But vi, which was already available on 2BSD (1979), only made it into a BTL distribution with v8 (1985).

Even in 1976, international communication and access to source meant the distribution of new tools and new programs encouraged and enlivened the user community. Let's look at the landscape for a few minutes.

- In 1974, Bob Kahn and Vint Cerf published the first paper describing what was to become TCP/IP.

- In 1975, RFC 681 was published.

- In January 1976, there were 63 hosts on the ARPANET, which was on the verge of becoming the Internet.

- And UNIX was available throughout the world — but only on machinery that cost well over $100,000.

The Daemon, the Gnu, and the Penguin

6 Communicating — UUCP and Usenet

Also in 1976, Mike Lesk[1] at AT&T developed UUCP (UNIX-to-UNIX copy). Version 2 was implemented in 1977.[2]

UUCP meant that information could be directed around the network (as it was). It also meant that one could establish a telephone connection and transmit information across that (relatively expensive) link. Two years later, three graduate students in North Carolina (Tom Truscott, Jim Ellis, and Steve Bellovin) took the next step.

Tom Truscott had an early interest in chess. While a student at Duke in 1974, he devised a chess program (Duchess) and played against Ken Thompson's Belle. Duchess lost on time. (In competitive chess, each side has a given time to make its next move; Duchess exceeded that time due to a core dump.) But Truscott competed in every ACM computer chess tournament from 1974 through 1980. He also attended the 1976 UNIX Users Group meeting at Harvard (1–2 April) and the 1978 meeting at Columbia (24–28 May), where he met Ken and others.[3] In 1979, Truscott went to the Labs as a summer student and, on his return

---

[1] Lesk earned a Ph.D. in Chemical Physics and worked in the UNIX group, where he wrote tbl, refer, lex, and UUCP. He went on to Bellcore; was head of a Division at the NSF (1998–2002); and is currently Professor of Library and Information Science at Rutgers.

[2] UUCP has a long history, see Chapter 15 of *Casting the Net*.

[3] This was the meeting at which the name was changed to USENIX, spurred by a letter from an AT&T lawyer stating that Western Electric had not given permission to use "UNIX" in "UNIX User Group." The lawyers were busily controlling the trademark, while the code was circulating (escaping?).

to Duke, arranged for a UUCP link. (He also attended the June 20–23 USENIX meeting in Toronto.)

When he returned to Duke, he found that Jim Ellis had installed V7 on the Computer Science PDP 11/70. They employed the auto-dialer capacity to dial up two other Duke computers and one at the University of North Carolina. Ellis and Truscott than called a meeting to discuss their idea — to have something like the mailing lists on the ARPANET for computer sites that weren't on the ARPANET. Steve Bellovin, then a graduate student at the University of North Carolina, attended and subsequently wrote the first Netnews program — three pages of shell script (later rewritten in C).

The first implementation was between the Duke and UNC Computer Science departments; the Duke Medical Center Department of Physiology (PHS) was added at the beginning of 1980. In January 1980, Ellis and Truscott went to Boulder, Colo., and announced their Netnews design at the USENIX meeting (January 29 — February 1). The first version of Netnews was fairly simple and efficient. It periodically checked the "last saved" time-stamp of each file in a specified directory, and then sent any file updated since the last check to another computer using UUCP across a modem connection. Machines typically "dialed up" the host machine several times a day to get whatever had accumulated.

Tom Truscott and Steve Daniel (also a graduate student at Duke) then rewrote the program to create what was called Netnews Version A. Since Netnews was designed for UNIX at a university, it was automatically categorized as public domain software under the conditions of the AT&T UNIX license, which greatly facilitated its subsequent use and adoption. This implementation appeared on the 1980 USENIX distribution tape, which was distributed at the Newark, Del., meeting (June 17–20). Duke University then invited other sites to join the network, which was made easier by the fact that the software was free, starting the first Usenet expansion – to 15 sites. But one of those was Berkeley, which caused an explosive growth spurt.[4]

That connection was the responsibility of Armando Stettner, who was then with DEC. Someone at the Delaware meeting complained about the inordinate cost of the long-distance telephone connections needed to get news to the West Coast. Armando spoke to Bill Shannon and they said that if they could get a news feed to decvax (in New Hampshire), they'd pick up the Berkeley phone bill. (Armando later supplied the first news feeds to Europe, Japan, and Australia, too.) The network soon spread to universities across North America, quickly establishing a critical mass of useful information, which made it even more popular.[5]

In under a year, Usenet grew to 100 sites and over 25 articles per day (the original protocol had been optimized for 1–2 messages per day). Mike Lesk had never contemplated such uses of uucp. Truscott, Ellis, and Bellovin had never imagined such popularity. The system collapsed.

In 1982, Netnews Version B was developed by Mark Horton (a graduate student at Berkeley) and Matt Glickman (a high school student) to increase efficiency so that it could cope with the increasing loads of the growing network. Horton continued to maintain the system till 1984, when Rick Adams at the Center for Seismic Studies took over maintenance of Version B, releasing 2.10.2. There were 135 news groups at the end of March. Version 2.11 of Netnews was released in late 1986.[6] In 1989, Netnews Version C was developed by Henry Spencer and Geoff Collyer at the University of Toronto to increase its efficiency again. But it was soon to be surpassed.

---

[4]Once more, "public domain" ensured the proliferation of a useful program.
[5]My 1986 business card had the email address:
{decvax,ucbvax}!usenix!peter.
[6]Rick (who was soon to go on to found UUNET), Spencer Thomas, Ray Essick, Rob Kolstad, and others continued to add useful features to Netnews.

The Daemon, the Gnu, and the Penguin

7 1979

In Chapter 4, UNIX V6, John Lions, and the ports of UNIX to the Interdata 7 and the Interdata 8 were mentioned. We're about to move on to V7. But first, a note about names and dates.

Names

By and large, UNIX users refer to "Sixth Edition" and "V6" interchangeably. As noted by Ken Thompson, at Bell Labs, there was a continually changing version of UNIX running. Only when Doug McIlroy caused the first "UNIX PROGRAMMER'S MANUAL" to be written, did there appear to be a fixed form. So, the manuals were listed by "Edition," and the system referred to was the "Version."

Dates

Every AT&T manual carried a date. The complete list of "Editions" is:[1]

- First Edition — November 3, 1971

- Second Edition — June 12, 1972

- Third Edition — February 1973

- Fourth Edition — November 1973

- Fifth Edition — June 1974

---

[1]There were, of course, other "UNIX" editions, e.g. *Programmer's Workbench* (PWB).

- Sixth Edition — May 1975

- Seventh Edition — January 1979

- Eighth Edition — February 1985

- Ninth Edition — September 1986

- Tenth Edition — October 1989

V7

The wonder of V6 was that it was under 10,000 lines of code. (But it had no full-screen editor, no windowing system, etc.) V7 was much larger. And it contained much more. V7 accommodated large filesystems; it did not restrict the number of user accounts; it had improved reliability. Steve Johnson referred to V7 as "the first portable UNIX." It also had a large number of new commands. Among these were

COMMANDS: at, awk, calendar, cb, cd, cpio, cu, deroff, expr, f77, find, lex, lint, m4, make, refer, sed, tail, tar, touch, uucp, uux

SYSTEM CALLS: ioctl

SUBROUTINES: malloc, stdio, string

GAMES: backgammon

awk (Aho-Weinberger-Kernighan)[2], lint (Johnson)[3], make (Feldman)[4], and uucp (Lesk) would have been enough, but there was much more. The V7 manual had grown to over 400 pages, with two 400-page supplementary volumes. V7 contained a full Kernighan-Ritchie C compiler; a far more sophisticated shell (sh), the Bourne shell; Dick Haight's find, cpio and expr; and a large number of include files.

Dated "January 1979," the title page of the Seventh Edition UNIX PROGRAMMER'S MANUAL bore neither Dennis' nor

---

[2] A pattern scanning and processing language; gawk (GNU AWK) is currently the most widely employed version.

[3] A C program verifier.

[4] A utility to simplify the maintenance of other programs.

Ken's name. It was headed: **UNIX**TM **TIME-SHARING SYS-TEM.**

Along with all this, V7 came with a major drawback: its performance was poorer than most V6 systems, especially those that had been "tuned." The users went to work. (After all, they had the source.)

Bill Joy (at Berkeley) changed the size of the data blocks on the VAX 11/780. (Jeff Schriebman ported that to the PDP-11/70 in April 1980, having gone to UniSoft from Berkeley.) In December 1979, Ed Gould moved the buffers out of kernel address space. Joy changed the stdio library on the VAX and Tom Ferrin (at UCSF) ported those changes to the PDP-11. Tom London (in Holmdel, N.J.) improved the movement of output characters from user space to kernel space. John Lions (at UNSW in Australia) proposed a new procedure for directory pathnames. UNSW also provided new code for process table matches. Bruce Borden (at the RAND Corporation) provided the symorder program. Ferrin also rewrote parts of copyseg() and clearseg(). The entire set of improvements was made available to the community on a PDP-11 distribution: 2.8.1BSD — it was announced by Ferrin at the USENIX Conference in January 1982 in Santa Monica, Calif.

The users had enhanced V7's performance dramatically.

But I've gone too far ahead.

USENIX

Ron Baecker of the University of Toronto hosted the USENIX Association meeting, June 20–23, 1979. There were about 400 attendees.

Al Arms, an AT&T lawyer, announced the new licensing terms for V7. In addition to a fee schedule that increased the costs of the various licenses, the academic/research license no longer automatically permitted unlimited classroom use. As Greg Rose (who was one of John Lions' students at UNSW and is now with Qualcomm) told me:

> It seems that in so many stages of UNIX's evolution, an action that AT&T took in order to stifle something actually caused the opposite to happen.
>
> Suppressing Lions' commentary led to wholesale distribution by Xerox copy. Here unthinking non-commercial pricing led to something truly unforeseen.

Andrew S. Tanenbaum of the Vrije Universiteit in Amsterdam had been using V6 in his classes on operating systems. It now appeared that he would not be able to employ V7. "It was the new licensing restrictions," he told me. And, as will be seen, Andy was driven to do something to alleviate the problem.

When AT&T released Version 7, it began to realize that UNIX was a valuable commercial product, so it issued Version 7 with a license that prohibited the source code from being studied in courses, in order to avoid endangering its status as a trade secret. Many universities complied by simply dropping the study of UNIX, and teaching only theory. (*Operating Systems*, 1987, p. 13.)

Andy was not to be deterred: he created an operating system like UNIX for use on Intel's new x86 architecture: MINIX.[5]

MIT

In 1974, Robert indexGreenblatt, RobertGreenblatt at the MIT AI Lab began the Lisp machine project. His first machine was called CONS (1975)[6]. This was improved into a version called CADR[7] (1977). CADR was the direct ancestor of both Lisp Machines,

---

[5] I'll discuss MINIX later. But some universities went along with AT&T: Clem Cole told me that he and Dan Klein had gone on "strike" at Carnegie Mellon until the university purchased a "full" $20,000 license.

[6] This was a pun on the list **construction** operator in Lisp.

[7] In Lisp, cadr returns the second element in a list.

Inc., of which Greenblatt was the founder and president, and of Symbolics, Inc. And Symbolics, in several ways, forced Richard Stallman to form the Free Software Foundation and the GNU Project.[8]

Berkeley

Though I will go into more detail concerning the Computing Systems Research Group (CSRG) at Berkeley in the next chapter, I think it important to note here that 3BSD, the first Berkeley UNIX release for the VAX, came out at the end of 1979. But this was not based on V7, but on 32V. Berkeley utilities and modifications from 2BSD (including the C shell) had been added, as well as a virtual memory system done by a number of Berkeley graduate students, including Bill Joy. It was an exciting year.

32V

Before going on to Berkeley, I should say something about 32V, the UNIX port to the DEC VAX (Virtual Address eXtension).

Nearly four years passed between V6 and V7. But, as I noted, things didn't stand still at the Labs. In fact, what we think of as V7 was available internally nearly a year prior to the publication of Seventh Edition.

Things hadn't remained static at DEC, either, and the first VAX, a 32-bit computer, was pre-announced in 1977 and went on sale in 1978. Dennis, Ken and Steve Johnson felt alienated by DEC. And Dennis and Steve were working on the port to the Interdata 8. So when DEC offered them a VAX, they just said "no." DEC then turned to Bell Labs in Holmdel. I spoke to Charlie Roberts, who was to manage the project.

> DEC came to us in Holmdel. We were clearly the second-string. Tom London and John Reiser were

---

[8]I'll discuss RMS, the FSF and GNU below.

interested and so was Ken Swanson, and we got the VAX in early '78. I didn't do any of the technical work. In fact, I devoted a lot of energy and time to getting the management to let us do it. It wasn't research you see. However, they let us take the time. And in about three months my small group ported Version 7 to the VAX. We got the machine in January; they had it running in April; and by August it really worked. By then folks knew what we were doing. I had had calls from about six universities — Brown, UCLA, Berkeley, Waterloo. I can't recall the others. So I went to Roy Lipton and Al Arms in Patents and Licensing about getting it out. After a lot of back-and-forth, they decided that we could give it to one university for research purposes and that Al would set up a "special research agreement" with that institution.

I had met [Bob] Fabry at a couple of conferences and I had been out in Berkeley and given a paper and talked to [Domenico] Ferrari as well as Emmanuel Blum and Bill Joy. So, with the blessings of BTL area 11 management, we sent 32V to Berkeley. It was in October or November 1978.

With that background, let's go cross country to Berkeley.

8 BSD and the CSRG

Professor Robert Fabry was on the program at the SOSP where Ken and Dennis delivered the first paper on UNIX. He was full of enthusiasm when he returned to Berkeley. When he got back to Cory Hall, his first chore was to attempt to assemble a joint purchase (by Computer Science, Math and Statistics) of a PDP-11/45.

He then ordered a tape from Thompson and, in January 1974, Keith Standiford (a graduate student) installed UNIX. As Kirk McKusick tells the tale, Ken had been involved in all the early installations – but not this one, "though his expertise was soon needed to determine the cause of several strange system crashes." Thompson would phone Keith in the machine room, the phone would be inserted in the 300 baud acoustic modem, and Ken would "remotely debug crash dumps from New Jersey."

The next problem arose because Math and Statistics wanted to run DEC's RSTS.[1] So slices of each day were allocated: eight hours for UNIX, followed by 16 hours for RSTS. One of the undergraduates introduced to UNIX at that time was Eric Allman.[2]

"I was taking an introductory OS course," he told me:

> and they had been using something called the Toy Operating System on the [CDC Cyber] 6400. But they wanted to get off it and on to UNIX on the 11/40[3], where we could only work eight hours a

---

[1] Resource Sharing Time Sharing Extended, a multi-user OS for the PDP-11 series, generally programmed in "Basic-Plus."

[2] Inventor of sendmail.

[3] The 11/40 was a higher-performance version of the 11/20. It was introduced

day, and a different eight hours each day. I recall
having difficulties. I was reading the manual, and I
remember not understanding why you would ever
want the echo command. Totally bizarre. Now, of
course, I know. Of course, 4th Edition was pretty
flaky. It was a system that only a researcher could
love. It was slow. It didn't have a lot of tools. Then I
got hired by the Ingres project.

The Ingres project of Professors Michael Stonebraker and Eugene Wong was one of the first projects moved to UNIX. As they were dissatisfied with the way time had been allocated, they bought their own PDP-11/40 in spring 1974. But there still wasn't enough student time available on the 11/45. In June 1974, Stonebraker and Fabry set out to get two instructional 11/45s for Computer Science. The money was obtained early in 1975, just about the time DEC announced the 11/70, which seemed more suitable (it was announced in March). So they pooled the money. The 11/70 arrived in fall 1975, just when Ken Thompson arrived for his one-year sabbatical as visiting professor. Thompson, Bob Kridle and Jeff Schriebman brought up V6 on the newly-installed 11/70. Adding the "50 bugs" tape was a side-effect.

That same autumn, two new graduate students arrived on the Berkeley campus: Chuck Haley and Bill Joy[4]. They were fascinated by V6 on the 11/70 and began working on the Pascal system that Ken had hacked together. In fact, Haley and Joy improved the Pascal system to the point that it became the system of choice for the students. And when the Model 33 Teletype terminals were replaced by ADM-3 screen terminals, they felt that

in January 1973. The 11/45 was a faster, microcoded 11/20, introduced in June 1972.

[4]Bill Joy received a degree in Electrical Engineering from the University of Michigan and a masters in EECS from UC Berkeley. After several years at the CSRG, Bill abandoned Ph.D. studies to become one of the founders of Sun (1982), whence he retired in 2003.

ed just wasn't good enough. So, as I've related, they developed ex from Coulouris' em.

Meanwhile, in a different part of the universe, Kirk McKusick, at that time a "JCL hacker" at Cornell, was exposed to UNIX by a friend who was studying at the University of Delaware. "He showed me how you could play games on it," McKusick told me,

> ... so I really didn't have any exposure to UNIX till I got out to Berkeley in 1976. I came out in the spring because I was looking at graduate programs to go to, and they were on spring break, so there weren't a lot of people around. But I came across Bill Joy in the computer room where he was busily hacking away and he said "Hi, I'm Bill Joy. This is what we're working on here—a Pascal system that runs under UNIX." And I said, "What can you do with UNIX?" So he said, "You can edit files and compile files and you can play chess. Let me log you in." So I proceeded to play chess the rest of the afternoon. And I decided that I liked Berkeley and that's where I'd go.

When Thompson returned to BTL at the end of the summer of 1976, Joy and Haley turned their interests toward the kernel. But word of the Pascal compiler got around. And at the beginning of 1978, Joy began producing the Berkeley Software Distribution (BSD). He offered a copy to Tom Ferrin (at UCSF) in a letter dated 9 March 1978. The "license" was on one side of a sheet of paper. Tom signed it on 13 March. The tape (in "standard tp format, 800 bpi ... ") consisted of:

a) UNIX Pascal system

b) Ex text editor

...

created by

a) W.N. Joy, S.L. Graham, C.B. Haley, K. Thompson

The Daemon, the Gnu, and the Penguin

b) W.N. Joy

Bill Joy, acting as "distribution secretary," sent out about 30 "free" copies of BSD in early 1978. By mid-year enough had been done (the Pascal system had been made more robust, the system could be run on the 11/34[5], and vi and termcap had been written[6]), that a "Second Berkeley Software Distribution" was put on tape.

Bill answered the phone, put together the distributions, and incorporated user feedback into the system. He also mailed out nearly 75 copies of 2BSD. 3BSD appeared in December 1979.

But during 1979 something else was proceeding at Berkeley.

The CSRG

Kirk McKusick has told the tale of the CSRG. Rather than rehash his narrative, here it is in his own words:

> In the fall of 1979, Bob Fabry responded to DARPA's interest in moving towards UNIX by writing a proposal suggesting that Berkeley develop an enhanced version of 3BSD for the use of the DARPA community. Fabry took a copy of his proposal to a meeting of DARPA image processing and VLSI contractors, plus representatives from Bolt, Beranek, and Newman, the developers of the ARPANET. There was some reservation whether Berkeley could produce a working system; however, the release of 3BSD in December 1979 assuaged most of the doubts.
>
> With the increasingly good reputation of the 3BSD release to validate his claims, Bob Fabry was able to get an 18-month contract with DARPA beginning

---

[5]The 11/34 was a cost-reduced version of the 11/35.

[6]vi was the result of the arrival of ADM-3a terminals; termcap was born when Joy decided to consolidate screen management, using an interpreter to redraw the screen.

in April 1980. This contract was to add features needed by the DARPA contractors. Under the auspices of this contract, Bob Fabry set up an organization which was christened the Computer Systems Research Group, or CSRG for short. He immediately hired Laura Tong to handle the project administration. Fabry turned his attention to finding a project leader to manage the software development. Fabry assumed that since Joy had just passed his Ph.D. qualifying examination, he would rather concentrate on completing his degree than take the software development position. But Joy had other other plans. One night in early March he phoned Fabry at home to express interest in taking charge of the further development of UNIX. Though surprised by the offer, Fabry took little time to agree.

The project started promptly. Tong set up a distribution system that could handle a higher volume of orders than Joy's previous distributions. Fabry managed to coordinate with Bob Guffy at AT&T and lawyers at the University of California to formally release UNIX under terms agreeable to all. Joy incorporated a variety of changes and 4BSD was released in October 1980.[7]

(The last CSRG system was 4.4BSD-Lite, Release 2, June 1995. Soon thereafter, the CSRG was disbanded. Another era was over.)

---

[7]Marshall Kirk McKusick, "20 Years of Berkeley UNIX: From AT&T-Owned to Freely Redistributable," Originally published in *Open Sources: Voices from the Open Source Revolution* http://www.oreilly.com/catalog/opensources/, 1st Edition, January 1999.

The Daemon, the Gnu, and the Penguin

9 "Free as in Freedom"

Richard M. Stallman (rms), though a freshman at Harvard, began working for Russ Noftsker at the MIT Artificial Intelligence Lab in 1971. While still in high school (The Adams School through junior year, senior year at Louis D. Brandeis on West 84th Street) in New York, he had worked briefly at the IBM Science Center and at Rockefeller University. As he put it:

> I became part of a software-sharing community that had existed for many years. Sharing of software was not limited to our particular community; it is as old as computers, just as sharing of recipes is as old as cooking. But we did it more than most.

> The AI Lab used a time-sharing operating system called ITS (the Incompatible Timesharing System) that the Lab's staff hackers had designed and written in assembler language for the Digital PDP 10 ... As a member of this community, an AI Lab staff system hacker, my job was to improve this system.

> We did not call our software "free software," because that term did not yet exist, but that is what it was. Whenever people from another university or a company wanted to port and use a program, we gladly let them. If you saw someone using an unfamiliar and interesting program, you could always ask to see the source code, so that you could read it, change it, or cannibalize parts of it to make a new program.[1]

---

[1] From *Free Software, Free Society* (FSF, 2002), p. 15.

Less than a decade later, everything changed for the worse. "It was Symbolics that destroyed the community of the AI Lab," rms told me. " Those guys no longer came to the Lab. In 1980 I spent three or four months at Stanford and when I got back [to Tech Square], the guys were gone. The place was dead." (Sam Williams says that Symbolics hired 14 AI Lab staff as part-time "consultants." Richard was truly the "last of the hackers.")

We see here what Richard wanted: a cooperative community of hackers, producing software that got better and better.

"In January '82 they [Symbolics] came out with a first edition," rms continued. "They didn't share. So I implemented a quite different set of features and rewrote about half of the code. That was in February. In March, on my birthday [March 16], war broke out. Everyone at MIT chose a side: *use* Symbolics' stuff, but not return source for development. I was really unhappy. The community had been destroyed. Now the whole attitude was changing."

In the essay cited above, rms continued:

> When the AI Lab bought a new PDP-10 in 1982, its administrators decided to use Digital's non-free time-sharing system instead of ITS.
>
> The modern computers of the era, such as the VAX or the 68020, had their own operating systems, but none of them were free software: you had to sign a nondisclosure agreement even to get an executable copy.
>
> This meant that the first step in using a computer was to promise not to help your neighbor. A cooperating community was forbidden. The rule made by the owners of proprietary software was, "If you share with your neighbor, you are a pirate. If you want any changes, beg us to make them."
>
> The idea that the proprietary software social system– the system that says you are not allowed to share

or change software–is antisocial, that it is unethical, that it is simply wrong, may come as a surprise to some readers. But what else could we say about a system based on dividing the public and keeping users helpless? Readers who find the idea surprising may have taken the proprietary social system as given, or judged it on the terms suggested by proprietary software businesses. Software publishers have worked long and hard to convince people that there is only one way to look at the issue . . . .

I have quoted Richard at length, because I think that his "voice" should be heard. He has frequently said that "Software should be free." But in 1982 and 1983 his was a single, lonely voice. He duplicated the work of the Symbolics programmers in order to prevent the company from gaining a monopoly. He refused to sign non-disclosure agreements, and he shared his work with others in what he still regards as the "spirit of scientific collaboration and openness." In September 1983, rms announced the GNU project. In January 1984 he resigned from his job at MIT. He has written:

I began work on GNU Emacs in September 1984, and in early 1985 it was beginning to be usable. This enabled me to begin using UNIX systems to do editing; having no interest in learning to use vi or ed, I had done my editing on other kinds of machines until then.

At this point, people began wanting to use GNU Emacs, which raised the question of how to distribute it. Of course, I put it on the anonymous ftp server on the MIT computer that I used. (This computer, prep.ai.mit.edu, thus became the principal GNU ftp distribution site; when it was decommissioned a few years later, we transferred the name to our new ftp server.) But at that time, many of the interested people were not on the Internet and could not get a copy by ftp. So the question was, what would I say to them?

I could have said, "Find a friend who is on the Net and who will make a copy for you." Or I could have done what I did with the original PDP-10 Emacs: tell them, "Mail me a tape and a SASE, and I will mail it back with Emacs on it." But I had no job, and I was looking for ways to make money from free software. So I announced that I would mail a tape to whoever wanted one, for a fee of $150. In this way, I started a free software distribution business, the precursor of the companies that today distribute entire Linux-based GNU systems.

That's it. In September 1983, the first draft of the *Manifesto* announced Richard's intent; just over a year later, his $150 GNU Emacs initiated an innovative business model.

Thanks to Patrick Henry Winston, director of the MIT AI Lab from 1972–1997, Richard's resignation didn't have the expected consequences. Winston allowed Stallman to continue to have office and lab space at Tech Square. The Lab's computing facilities were also available for Richard's use. And when (in 2004) MIT opened its new computer building, Richard M. Stallman was given office space.

Let me now move back in time and across the Atlantic.

Excursus: Hardware

J. C. R. Licklider wrote that computers were communication devices, not calculating devices. Tomlinson's creation of email (1970) was a step demonstrating that. The continued expansion of the Internet provided the medium. UUCP and Usenet provided further impetus.

In January 1976, there were 63 hosts on the Internet. Five years later, there were just over 200. In August 1982, there were 235. For nearly 20 years thereafter, the number of Internet host sites doubled yearly: 562 in August 1983; 1024 in October 1984; 2308 in February 1986; 28,174 in December 1987; 727,000 in January 1992. But the slope of that curve has flattened. We no longer talk about hosts; we talk about users. But that's hard to estimate. How many people own a domain ... or several domains? And how many users are "on" some major domains? And what's the average? So it's largely guesswork. Around 2002, there appeared to be about 300 to 500 million users of the Internet. Right now, perhaps a sixth of mankind has access.

Two factors drove this (in my opinion): the development of the modem and the affordable personal computer.[1]

A modem (**mo**dulator-**dem**odulator) sends and receives data between two computers. The first commercial modem, the Bell 103, was built by AT&T in 1962. It had full duplex transmission, frequency-shift keying and operated at 300 bits per second. Things got a bit speedier over time: 1200 bps, 9600 bps, 14,400bps. Robert Lucky invented the "automatic adaptive

---

[1] This Excursus is not intended to be a complete, formal history: my intent is to offer enough background information to make the subsequent chapters more intelligible.

equalizer" at Bell Labs in 1965. Brent Townshend, a Quebec inventor, invented the 56K pulse-core-modulated modem in 1996. Things had gotten a lot better.

Personal workstations and personal computers are not new, either. I can recall the LINC of 1963, for example. But these machines, as well as PERLIS and the early HP calculators, though of historical importance, had little impact on where we are now.

But we do need to look back at the 1976 Apple 1, 1MHz 8kB RAM (max. 32KB); the Apple][(1977), the][e (1983), and the Macintosh SE (1987), because they did have an impact on the industry. And they had their beginnings in the Altair.

In 1973 and 1974 a small company in Albuquerque, N.Mex., called MITS (Micro Instrumentation Telemetry Systems), which had been producing inexpensive calculators, was seeking a new product. Texas Instruments had just taken over its calculator market. Ed Roberts, with the help of Les Solomon, decided to build a computer kit. Assisted by two hardware engineers, William Yates and Jim Bybee, they developed the MITS Altair[2] 8800, which was featured on the cover of the January 1975 *Popular Electronics*. The magazine called the Altair the "World's First Minicomputer Kit to Rival Commercial Models." It shipped for $400, but the purchaser had to assemble it, get it to work, and write the necessary software. It wasn't all fun, but it sold.

Among others, it sold to a Harvard freshman, Bill Gates, and his friend Paul Allen. They compiled a version of BASIC to run on the Altair. (Roberts offered Allen the post of Director of Software at MITS — he was the only person in the department. Gates joined him in Albuquerque after he left Harvard.)

The Apple][e ran on a SynerTek 6502 board. The SE was 8MHz, 256kB, ran on the Motorola 68000, and had a serial port into which a modem could be plugged. It sold for just under $3000. (As I was Executive Director of USENIX in 1987, Telebit gave me a Qblazer and I connected the SE from home to the

---

[2]The Altair was named by Solomon's 12-year-old daughter, after a *Star Trek* episode.

office using RedRider.) Real power. And there were nearly 300 groups on Usenet.

But in 1975, IBM had tried to enter the "small machine" market with its 5100 — a 50-pound "portable" computer, priced at $9000 to $20,000. It was a dismal flop. (Remember: "There is no reason anyone would want a computer in their home," Ken Olsen, founder of DEC, said in 1977, echoing Alexander Graham Bell who had said, a century earlier, that no one would want a telephone in their home. Our crystal balls are murky.) IBM then contemplated buying up Atari, but instead set up an "independent business unit" in Boca Raton, Fla., to build the"Acorn."[3] The team of a dozen engineers was headed by William C. Lowe. They made a number of unusual decisions, the most notable of which was that the PC would have open, rather than proprietary architecture. They also decided to save time by purchasing an operating system, as well as making hardware components open to competitive bids. Finally, the PCs were to be sold through retail channels.

Released in August 1981, the original PC ran on a 4.77MHz Intel 8088. It had 16kB of memory, expandable to 256kB. It was priced at $1565 and launched through a brilliant advertising campaign featuring a Charlie Chaplin look-alike. By 1985, IBM's sales had overtaken Apple's and IBM had 40% PC market share.

However, the very open architecture that made the IBM PC a success, led to its decline. Open architecture meant that others could clone it, and the first of these was Compaq, coming out with an 80386-based machine in 1986. Others followed. By 1995, IBM's market share had dropped to 7.3% and in 2003 it was 6%. IBM then sold off its PC business to Lenovo.

In 1981, the Osborne 1, the first true portable had been released. It had 64K RAM; twin 5.25", 91K drives; and ran on a Zilog Z80 at 4MHz. It was followed by the Osborne 2 and then the Osborne 3, which existed in prototype, but was never

---

[3]See Pugh, *Building IBM*, pp. 313f., and P.E. Ceruzzi, *A History of Modern Computing*, 2nd Ed. (MIT Press, 2003), pp. 268–273.

released. Though the company eventually failed, the machines were definite landmarks.[4]

---

[4] Adam Osborne (1939–2003) was born in Thailand of British parents and attended Birmingham University and the University of Delaware. He worked for Shell for a while, founded a series of readable manuals and sold the publishing endeavor, Osborne Books, to McGraw Hill in 1977. At that point he obtained some backing and, with engineer Lee Felsenstein, founded Osborne Computer. His autobiography, *Hypergrowth: The Rise and Fall of the Osborne Computer Corporation* (with John C. Dvorak), 1984, is well worth reading.

10 MINIX

Like Richard Stallman, Andy Tanenbaum was born in New York. After graduating from high school in White Plains (just north of New York City), he went to MIT, and subsequently received his doctorate from Berkeley. Since 1971 he has lived in the Netherlands (his wife is Dutch) where he's Professor of Computer Science at the Vrije Universiteit (Free University, VU).

After AT&T's 1979 announcement of the V7 licensing restrictions, precluding the use of the code in classrooms, Andy decided that the solution lay in his "helping himself."

Together with Sape Mullender, of the CWI (Center for Mathematics and Computer Science), Andy had originated the Amoeba project. Amoeba was one of the earliest attempts at a distributed operating system, contemporary with Roger Needham's work in Cambridge, and preceding LOCUS, CHORUS, V, and Mach. (Tanenbaum & Mullender, in *Operating Systems Review* 13(2): 26–32, 1981.) That same year, Andy's valuable *Computer Networks* (Prentice-Hall) appeared.

And, while doing research, teaching classes, supervising graduate students, and writing, Andy worked on his own system. "It took about two years," he told me. He called it MINIX.

MINIX was a micro-kernel UNIX clone. While it emulated UNIX, it contained no AT&T code — not in the kernel, not in the compiler, not in the utilities. It was 1986. The next year, 1987, *Operating Systems: Design and Implementation* came out, the book's title reflecting the VU course that Andy was teaching. At first, the code (v1.1) was available on diskettes from Prentice-Hall. Soon it was available without the book.

MINIX 1.3 was on five 1.2M floppies and cost $60; MINIX

1.5 (1991) came on 12 720K diskettes at $169. 1.5 contained the accumulated bug fixes; it was V7 system call compatible; it would run on the IBM PC, PC AT, PC XT, PS/2, and 286/386 as well being "available" for the Atari ST, the Macintosh, the Amiga, and the Sun SparcStation 1, 1+, or IPC. 1.5 had a K&R compatible C compiler, a Bourne-like shell, five editors (ed, ex, an Emacs subset, a vi clone, and "a simple screen editor"), and a great deal of other goodies.

MINIX was intended as a teaching tool, and it was far from freely redistributable. It was under copyright by Prentice-Hall, but with rather liberal copy and revise/extend restrictions. However, it was certainly not free. As I understand it, the Prentice-Hall lawyers are to blame here, not Andy. MINIX now is free: the license has been redone and made retroactive. MINIX 2 and MINIX 3 are freely redistributable software.

11 SUN and GCC

The company we think of as Sun Microsystems began with Andreas Bechtolsheim and some other graduate students at Stanford emulating Motorola's 68000 CPU cheaply. Stanford licensed a single board: the Stanford University Network board — SUN.

Soon, companies began licensing the board: Codata, Fortune, Dual, Cyb, Lucasfilm, and others. Machines began appearing. Each was "just another workstation" — JAWS.

The first UNIX workstation had been the Z8000 ONYX, hardly a VAX on a chip. John Bass demo-ed it at the USENIX Conference in Boulder, Colo., 29 January to 1 February 1980. "The system we took to Boulder was on three boards about 15 by 22 inches," Bass told me.

> Its performance and architecture was more like a PDP-11/45 or 11/70 ... segmented memory, no paging .... That aside, the ONYX was the first table-top system designed to run UNIX. With eight serial ports [users] and at under $25k, it made a great short-term alternative to PDP-11 UNIX systems.

But then came those JAWS — some of them at under $10K. And all of them ran AT&T's System III or 4.1BSD.

System III was AT&T's commercial variety of V7. Though its official release date was 31 October 1981, it reached some of the purchasers earlier and the general public in 1982.

Berkeley[1] issued 4BSD in October 1980. It included a faster file system, job control, auto reboot, delivermail (soon to be renamed

---

[1] I owe most of the BSD version chronology to Keith Bostic.

sendmail), and Franz Lisp. In June 1981, 4.1BSD, which had autoconfiguration and some minor improvements, was issued. Just why it was 4.1 (leading to 4.1a, 4.1b, 4.1c, 4.2, 4.3, and 4.4) is another of the silly consequences that licensing restrictions force upon developers.

Bill Joy made a 10-day visit to DEC in early 1981, working with Armando Stettner (who had gone to DEC from Bell Labs as "a sort of UNIX ambassador") on porting 4BSD to the VAX.

> We made a dump tape [Armando told me] and Bill packed up and went back to California. [Bill] Shannon and I took the disk pack and brought it up on decvax — a 780, our main system. Bill Joy called a couple of days later and said, "Hey, there's going to be a lot of hassle with the license if we do another release. So why don't we call it 4.1BSD?"

4.1a, 4.1b, and 4.1c were all "test releases." 4.1a included TCP/IP and the socket interface and was sent to a number of ARPANET sites. 4.1b included the new "fast file system." and new networking code. It was only used once on the Berkeley campus, in a graduate OS class. 4.1c was almost 4.2BSD, lacking only the new signal facility. It was sent to about 100 sites.

System III was distributed by AT&T without source. It was the first version of UNIX to be issued that way. But those customers who were unhappy merely obtained V7 from Western Electric or used the Berkeley editions ... which came with source.

The June 1982 issue of *;login:* (the newsletter of the USENIX Association) carried an article headlined:

Interesting Developments: Bill Joy of UCB moving to Sun Microsystems

Bill took a tape of 4.1cBSD with him. It became the basis for SunOS.[2] 4.2BSD became DEC's Ultrix.

---

[2]SUN was always a UNIX company, but the SUN-1 ran UniSoft's V7.

For half-a-dozen years, improvements in BSD were incorporated into subsequent versions of SunOS. But in 1988 AT&T announced a major investment in Sun Microsystems and thereby startled the UNIX community. (Ostensibly, the purpose was to merge the AT&T and Berkeley strains of UNIX. Most saw a far darker purpose.)

gcc

The GNU C Compiler (gcc) was Richard Stallman's first free software "hit." There were many C compilers available (at least four or five of them written by Whitesmiths, P.J. Plauger's software company[3]), but they were all proprietary. Stallman's was unencumbered — and it worked well. (gcc now stands for GNU Compiler Collection, and comprises compilers for C, C++, Objective-C, Fortran, Java, Ada, and a large number of libraries; a two-CD set still costs only $45.)

Remember, the USENIX community had been issuing free distribution tapes for a decade, and Rich Morin, one of the founders of the Sun User Group, had emulated this practice. When Stallman's compiler came out in 1987, Morin recognized that the hassles he had encountered in getting permissions from contributors were resolved by the GPL. And he recognized that the GPL made what he was engaged in a possible business. Morin's "service" became his company: Prime Time Freeware.

In 1990 I became Executive Director of the Sun User Group. In December I headed for San Jose for SUG's Eighth Annual Conference and Exhibit. It was a very tense meeting. In the first few hours I was at the hotel and the Convention Center, I became aware of the fact that there were two separate (though overlapping) sets of highly irate users.

One of these was made up of those who had bought a Sun 386i, Sun's sole venture into the Intel world. Though it was a business failure, the decision to end support for the machine was

[3]See my interview with Plauger, *Quarter Century of UNIX*, pp. 174–176.

not greeted with huzzahs. At the "Meet the Executives" session, Ed Zander explained that Sun wasn't "abandoning" the users and that an external firm would support the 386i for (as I recall it) "up to five years." The faithful were not appeased.

The second group were irate because Sun had "unbundled" its software. That is, rather than getting all of Sun's developer tools together, they had to be purchased separately. And of course, they cost more this way.

But wait. Why purchase the C compiler from Sun, when you could get a better one for less money from the FSF? That's what a large number of Sun's users asked themselves. And the net result was a real jump in CD sales at the FSF. (Several years later, when I organized the Freely Redistributable Software conference (February 1996) and then became Vice President of the FSF, I realized more fully just how much Sun had benefited the FSF. I'm certain this was not a foreseen consequence.)

The GNU C compiler was not the first piece of freely redistributable software, but it was the first widely circulated product of Stallman's project.

Excursus: UUNET

By the mid-1980s there were several commercial networks in operation. But they were limited in service and, generally quite high in price. None was what we would think of as an ISP.

In the Autumn of 1985, Rick Adams (then at "seismo"), approached Debbie Scherrer, vice-president of USENIX, with a plan for a centralized site, accessed via Tymnet by subscribers, supplying Usenet access.[1] In an email dated December 6, 1985, Debbie expressed interest in this.

Rick attended the October 1986 USENIX Board meeting in Monterey, Calif., where reaction was mixed, one director asking why folks would pay for access that could be obtained free. But the Board agreed to entertain a formal proposal. Rick brought a brief plan to the January 1987 (Washington, D.C.) meeting.

A majority of the USENIX Board liked the plan, but it really wasn't much of a formal "business plan," and Rick was asked to fill it out, with the participation of Board members John Quarterman and Wally Wedel, and return. By late March 1987 (in New Orleans), Rick was back with a full business plan and the Board approved it enthusiastically. I was authorized to spend up to $35,000 for an experimental period.

At that time I was Executive Director of the USENIX Association. I handled the UUNET application for not-for-profit status,

---

[1] Tymnet was an early proprietary network, first set up parallel to the ARPANET by Tymshare, Inc., using Interdata 7/32s as nodes. In 1979, Tymnet was spun off by Tymshare and bought up by McDonnell-Douglas in 1984. In 1989, BT North America bought Tymnet from McDonnell-Douglas. In 1993, MCI bought Tymnet from BT North America for stock. Tymnet survived MCI's acquisition by WorldCom, but was finally closed down in 2004.

the liaison with the lawyer, and signed all the checks for about 14 months. Over that period, the USENIX Board increased its "advance" to over $100,000. In only a few years, UUNET repaid all its debt.

UUNET was born.

"As people moved from universities and corporations, where they had email and Usenet access, to jobs where they had no access," Rick told me, "a need developed for a service that could provide email and Usenet access.

"UUNET was created in response to that need."

When the word got out, the demand far exceeded expectations. For example, Rick and Mike O'Dell had forecast 50 subscribers by the "end of summer." They topped 50 by mid-June 1987. Five years later, they had several thousand customers. UUNET reincorporated as a for-profit and then had its IPO (Initial Public Offering). There is a long and interesting history, involving MCI and WorldCom; but this is not the place for it. The important thing is that Rick's and Mike's vision was instantiated and proved valid: UUNET initiated commercial delivery of Usenet and the Internet.

Yet another thread in the communications part of our fabric.

12 OSF and UNIX International

In 1987, AT&T purchased a sizable percentage of Sun Microsystems and there was a joint announcement that they would be involved in a grand merger of System V and BSD. Moreover, AT&T announced that Sun would receive "preferential treatment" as AT&T/USL (UNIX Systems Laboratories) developed new software. Sun announced that its next operating system would not be a further extension of SunOS.

The scientific community felt that Sun was turning its back on them. The manufacturers felt that the special relationship would mean that Sun would get the jump on them. Great cries of praise did not go up from the computer manufacturers. "When Sun and AT&T announced the alliance," Armando Stettner told me,

> we at Digital were concerned that AT&T was no longer the benign, benevolent progenitor of UNIX ...Sun was everyone's most aggressive competitor. We saw that Sun's systems were direct replacements for the VAX. Just think: the alliance combined our most aggressive and innovative competitor with the sole source of the system software — the balance shifted.

There was a meeting at DEC's Western Offices in Palo Alto, Calif. There were participants from Apollo, DEC, Gould Electronics, Hewlett-Packard, Honeywell-Bull, InfoCorp, MIPS, NCR, Silicon Graphics, UniSoft, and Unisys. The group (called "the

Hamilton Group," because DEC's building was at 100 Hamilton Avenue) sent a telegram to James E. Olson, CEO of AT&T, requesting a meeting "during the week of January 25" with Vittorio Cassoni (Senior VP of AT&T's Data Systems Division).

Larry Lytel of HP called a preliminary meeting of the group at the JFK Marriott for the evening of 27 January. The meeting with Cassoni took place the next day. There was a follow-up meeting of the Hamilton Group in Dallas on 9 February. The meeting with Cassoni had had no positive effect where the Group was concerned. (It's not clear whether AT&T took the Group seriously. It appears that Cassoni just thought of this as jockeying for commercial advantage.) In March, IBM was invited to join.

Apollo, DEC, HP, IBM, Bull, Nixdorf, and Siemens held semi-secret meetings and in May 1988, the formation of the Open Software Foundation (OSF) was announced. (*The Wall Street Journal* for May 18 noted that no one present at the launch of OSF could recall ever seeing Ken Olsen sharing a stage with an IBM chief executive.)

Ken Thompson was in Australia at the time. When Ritchie told him what had transpired, he said: "Just think, IBM and DEC in one room and we did it!"

The seven companies listed above were joining hands to produce a new UNIX kernel and a new user interface. Their "temporary" headquarters would be in Lawrence, Mass. A delegation of executives (loaned to OSF from their various corporations) attended the USENIX Conference in San Francisco in June.

It didn't take long for AT&T, Sun and their coterie to form a counter-consortium: UNIX International (UI), dedicated to the marketing of SVR4.

OSF quickly named its executive team, including David Tory (Computer Associates) as President; and Roger Gourd (DEC), Ira Goldstein (HP), and Alex McKenzie (IBM) among the Vice Presidents.

UI appointed Peter Cunningham (International Computers, Ltd.) as President.

By the end of 1989, Gourd's engineering team had come out with a new user interface, Motif, which was well-received, and Goldstein's research team had chosen Mach as the underlying kernel for the new OS. OSF also increased its number of sponsors, adding Hitachi and Philips. However, as HP swallowed up Apollo and Siemens bought Nixdorf, at year end there were still seven sponsors.

Both OSF and UI ran membership drives and gave out pens and badges and stickers. Each ended up with about 200 members.

In 1991–92 the worldwide economy worsened. Bull, DEC, IBM, and the computer side of Siemens all lost money. AT&T resold its share of Sun. The fierce mudslinging appeared to be over. (At one point there was even a rumor of OSF and UI merging, for the good of UNIX.)

It hardly seemed to matter: Sun had adopted Motif; in 1993 USL sold UNIX to Novell, whereupon UI disbanded; OSF abandoned several of its previously announced products (shrink-wrapped software and the distributed management environment); Bull, Philips and Siemens withdrew from sponsorship of OSF.

Armando remarked to me: "It's not clear whether there's any purpose to OSF any more."

In 1984 a group of UNIX vendors had formed a consortium, X/Open, to sponsor standards. It was incorporated in 1987 and based in London. In 1996 OSF merged with X/Open to become The Open Group.

X/Open owned the UNIX trademark, which passed on to The Open Group. The Group also took on Motif and the Common Desktop Environment (CDE).

But the Open Group also maintained its concern with standards, and is the sponsor of the Single UNIX Specification. It has also taken on sponsorship of other standards including CORBA and the Linux Standard Base.

The Daemon, the Gnu, and the Penguin

13 GNU, the GPL and Cygnus

In September 1983, there was an "announcement." Then, in 1984, Richard Stallman issued *The GNU Manifesto*. In my opinion, it marks the true beginning of the GNU Project.

For several years, the Manifesto was updated repeatedly in minor ways, but it remained the primary document through which rms would "ask for participation and support."

Stallman and his small group of programmers had been working on rms' stated goal of free versions of all the UNIX applications and tools. By mid-1984, there were

> an Emacs text editor with Lisp for writing editor commands, a source-level debugger, a yacc-compatible parser generator, a linker, and around 35 utilities. A shell (command interpreter) is nearly completed. A new portable optimizing C compiler has compiled itself and may be released this year. An initial kernel exists but many more features are needed to emulate UNIX .... We will use TeX as our text formatter, but an nroff is being worked on ....

It was pretty impressive.

I'm not going to quote much more of the *Manifesto*, but there is one part, "Why I must write GNU," that has been my "favorite" for twenty years.

> I consider that the golden rule requires that if I like a program I must share it with other people who like

it. Software sellers want to divide the users and con-
quer them, making each user agree not to share with
others. I refuse to break solidarity with other users in
this way. I cannot in good conscience sign a nondis-
closure agreement or a software license agreement.
For years I worked within the Artificial Intelligence
Lab to resist such tendencies and other inhospitali-
ties, but eventually they had gone too far. I could not
remain in an institution where such things are done
for me against my will.

So that I can continue to use computers without dis-
honor, I have decided to put together a sufficient
body of free software so that I will be able to get
along without any software that is not free. I have resigned from the AI lab to deny MIT any legal excuse
to prevent me from giving GNU away.

Take this seriously. Just over twenty years ago, rms was talking about a political and social movement. He was talking about
"solidarity" and "conscience." This was a *Manifesto* in the same
sense that that of Marx and Engels was in 1848.

This was truly "cooperation." It was for the good of the larger
community.

Stallman was more interested in "freedom than in having a
better program"[1]. Hey! Not a bad outlook! I really like (say)
the most recent Tom Clancy, so I lend it to a friend. This week's
cartoon in *The Economist* strikes me, so I clip it and send it to a
pal. But, if it's software? Fugeddaboutit!

Stallman also produced the GPL — the GNU Public License,
now the GNU General Public License. The GPL grew out of a
real need for for legal documentation.

James Gosling, then a graduate student at Carnegie Mellon,
wrote a C-based version of Emacs which used a simplified Lisp,

---

[1]Interview with Michael Gross, "early 1999"; in *The More Things Change* (Harper
Collins, 2000).

MOCKLISP. In order to construct GNU Emacs on Lisp, rms freely borrowed Gosling's innovations. (Stallman had been told by other CMU developers that Gosling had assured their work on GOSMACS and the Lisp interpreter would remain available. But Gosling put GOSMACS under copyright and sold the rights to UniPress. UniPress, in turn, threatened to sue rms.)

As Sam Williams put it,

> Once again, Stallman faced the prospect of building from the ground up.
>
> In the course of reverse-engineering Gosling's interpreter, Stallman would create a fully functional Lisp interpreter, rendering the need for Gosling's original interpreter moot. Nevertheless, the notion of developers selling off software rights — indeed, the very notion of developers having software rights to sell in the first place — rankled Stallman.[2]

GNU Emacs was released in 1985, but rms had come to realize just how important it would be for GNU software to have a "legal foundation" to stand upon. The first version of the GPL was the direct result. Richard had realized that one needed to actually bestow an absolute right on users. He had spoken with Mark Fischer, a Boston IP lawyer, and to Jerry Cohen, another lawyer, but wrote his own license. Only a few years later, GPL version 2 was released. This was in 1991. Just about 15 years later, many still use that version, though version 3, released in 2007, is gaining adherents.

If you're curious, look at the copyright notice in the README file of trn (threaded read news), written by Larry Wall, prior to the creation of Perl. It says:

---

[2]Sam Williams, *Free as in Freedom* (O'Reilly, 2002), pp. 104f.

The Daemon, the Gnu, and the Penguin

Copyright (c) 1985, Larry Wall

You may copy the trn kit in whole or in part as long as you don't

try to make money off it, or pretend that you wrote it.

Yep.

In 1991 there was no Web.

In 1991 there was no Linux.

In 1991 KDE, Gnome, Apache, Netscape, hadn't even been thought of.

In 1991 we were still waiting for the Hurd.

But John Gilmore, employee number 5 at Sun Microsystems, was aware of the importance of GNU and of the GPL. Gilmore was part of the Usenet community. He was more than just a reader of net news. In November 1986, Gilmore suggested that rms "remove 'EMACS' from the license and replace it with 'SOFTWARE' or something." Version 1.0 of the GPL was officially released in 1989, a year after the release of the GNU debugger, which carried the 1985 draft (emended innumerable times).

Another individual taken by the GNU philosophy was Michael Tiemann. In an essay published in 1999, Tiemann looked back at the *Manifesto*: "It read like a socialist polemic, but I saw something different: I saw a business plan in disguise."[3] He dropped out of the Ph.D. program at Stanford to pursue that plan. Tiemann wrote the GNU C++ compiler and the first native-code C++ compiler and debugger. He is now Vice President for Open Source Affairs at Red Hat.

In 1989, Gilmore, Tiemann and David Henkel-Wallace cofounded Cygnus Solutions, the first "open source" business. (I put "open source" in quotation marks to differentiate it from free

---

[3]In *Open Sources* (O'Reilly, 1999), p. 139.

source. Stallman notes that "open source" stresses the technical side of the software, excellence through code sharing, whereas "free software" emphasizes the moral and ethical, technical excellence being a desirable byproduct.) Gilmore ceased working at Cygnus in 1995 and stepped down from its Board in 1997.

Cygnus was founded on the theory that "There is great value in having good people working on software whose precedents will set the standards of tomorrow. We believed at the beginning that people would understand this value proposition, and would value the opportunity to pay us to create high-quality, open-source programs that would become the *de facto* standard of the software world."[4]

Cygnus began by selling the GNU compiler and debugger as shrink-wrapped software. Gilmore sent out email telling folks that he'd be the debugger maintainer and integrator. Gilmore and Gumby (D.V. Henkel-Wallace) hacked and Tiemann sold contracts.

Cygnus became a success: it demonstrated that money could be made through service, packaging and distributing source that was otherwise free.

All the vision of Stallman and the hard work of Gilmore, Gumby and Tiemann bore fruit in Cygnus' GNUPro Developers Kit, which contained:

- GCC

- G++

- GDB

- GAS (GNU Assembler)

- LD (GNU Linker)

- Cygwin (UNIX Environment for Windows)

---

[4]Tiemann, Ibid.

- Insight (GUI for GDB)
- Source-Navigator

By the early 1990s, the world was really beginning to change.

14 USL v The Regents of the University of California

From late 1986 on, Keith Bostic would stand up at each USENIX Conference and announce the progress of his — the CSRG's — project: ridding Berkeley UNIX of AT&T code. About 35% of the code was AT&T license free; about 55%; about 77% ... The progress may have seemed slow at times, but there was always some progress.

And there were always loud cheers and resounding applause.

AT&T's lawyers had started off on the wrong foot in the mid-1970s; the fee structure made AT&T-license free UNIX a financial necessity. Among others, John Gilmore nudged the CSRG to produce a license-free version. After all, it was clear that AT&T hadn't objected to MINIX, which was a UNIX-like system with no AT&T code.

In November 1988, at the BSD Workshop in Berkeley, Keith, Mike Karels and Kirk McKusick announced the completion and availability of BSD Networking Release 1.

NET 1 was a subset of the then-current Berkeley system. It was quite similar to 4.3-Tahoe, including source code and documentation for the networking portions of the kernel, the C library and utility programs. It was available without evidence of any prior license (AT&T or Berkeley), and was (re)distributed via anonymous FTP. The source carried a Berkeley copyright notice and a legend that allowed redistribution with attribution.

(The Berkeley license was, and still is, different from the GPL.

The Daemon, the Gnu, and the Penguin

Keith and rms had debated the various aspects of the licenses repeatedly, without convergence. I will discuss this later.)

In June 1991, at the USENIX Conference in Nashville, BSD Networking Release 2 was available. NET 2 contained far more than just networking code and, like NET 1, was available with no prior license. The new features included a new virtual memory system (derived from Carnegie-Mellon's Mach system, which had been ported at the University of Utah) and a port to the Intel 386/486.

It was nearly the end of the line for the CSRG. Karels left Berkeley in 1992; Bostic and McKusick, in June 1993. But, NET 2 was a US-Russia collaboration, with contributions by Bill Jolitz, Donn Seeley, Trent Hein, Vadim Antonov, Mike Karels, Igor Belchinsky, Pace Willisson, Jeff Polk, and Tony Sanders. It was turned into a commercial product, known as BSDI (Berkeley Software Design, Inc.) and was complete by the end of 1991 and released to the public on April 10, 1993 as 1.0, the long delay being the consequence of UNIX Systems Laboratories (USL) filing suit to prevent BSDI from shipping its product.

USL filed for an injunction barring distribution of "BSD/386, pending trial, arguing that BSD/386 infringed USL's copyright in its 32V software and misappropriated USL trade secrets." [The story of 32V is in Chapter 7, above.] The Court denied USL's request for a preliminary injunction on March 3, 1993, ruling that USL had "failed to show a likelihood of success on either its copyright claim or its trade secret claim."

On March 30, 1993, Judge Dickinson Debevoise of the US District Court of New Jersey reaffirmed his denial of USL's motion for a preliminary injunction against BSDI. The Court found that the 32V source code had been distributed without a copyright notice. The Court rejected USL's argument that the publication of 32V was sufficiently limited to avoid a forfeiture, and thus found that USL had failed to establish that BSD/386 contained any USL trade secrets.

USL subsequently filed a motion for reconsideration, asking

the District Court to hold a new hearing on whether USL had published 32V without a copyright notice. USL argued that the Court's prior ruling was based on an incorrect finding as to the number of copies distributed. (USL's motion for reconsideration did not challenge the Court's ruling that USL had failed to establish trade secret misappropriation.)

The Court denied USL's motion for reconsideration. Although the Court amended its prior factual finding as to the number of copies distributed, it found that the number was not critical to its ruling on the issue of publication without notice.

It was just under 20 years since Ken had delivered that first UNIX paper at SOSP and began receiving requests for the software. It was 15 years since *UNIX NEWS* became *;login:* and the "UNIX Users Group" turned into USENIX. And, through all of this, Western Electric, AT&T, and now USL had learned nothing about the nature of the user community.

What BSDI (and other companies, like mt Xinu) were trying to do was ensure the continued development, growth and use of the UNIX operating system. The suit by USL was an attempt to protect something of value. But that value had been discovered too late.

Perhaps Ritchie and Thompson had handled the system carelessly in the mid-1970s; maybe BTL employees inadvertently gave UNIX to the public without any significant restriction. But the users, like O'Dell and Kolstad, Coulouris and Lions, Tanenbaum and Joy had seen the value. That value was not merely the thousands of lines of code, but the tens of thousands of users — who contributed to the further development of the code.

BSDI had distributed pre-production releases of BSD/386 (Beta version). It now began international distribution. Full source was priced at $1000. (In the January/February 1994 *;login:*, Lou Katz wrote: "It works! It works!").

Because of the way the licenses had been granted to the University of California, the Regents of the University had been included in USL's suit. In June 1993, the Regents struck back, filing suit against USL for not complying with agreements made with the CSRG.

In the meantime, Novell acquired USL. A decade later, it is still unclear exactly what USL believed it was selling, nor what Novell thought it was buying.

To take but one example, the "PROPRIETARY NOTICE" on the System V errno.h file reads:

> This source code is unpublished proprietary information constituting, or derived under license from AT&T's UNIX (r) System V. In addition, portions of such source code were derived from Berkeley 4.3 BSD under license from the Regents of the University of California.

USL had filed suit in New Jersey, the home of AT&T and Bell Labs (and USL), clearly thinking that this would yield a "home team" advantage in their suit. When the USL v BSDI and Regents suit was dismissed, the Regents filed suit in California.

On Friday, February 4, 1994, Novell and the University of California mutually agreed to drop all relevant suits and counter-suits. BSDI immediately announced the availability of a release based on "4.4BSD-Lite."

"We are delighted to settle with USL so that we can devote our full efforts to creating products and serving our customers," Rob Kolstad, president of BSDI, said to me.

There is no question that The Open Group "owns" the UNIX trademark. There are many questions as to whether any one entity "owns" UNIX. In 1995, Novell executed an "Asset Purchase Agreement" with the Santa Cruz Operation, though exactly what was purchased is unclear over a decade later.

While both The SCO Group (a successor to the Santa Cruz Operation) and Novell claim rights to the UNIX source code, many elements of that code carry copyright notices from the University of California and other companies and individuals.

All of this is important because of the various suits filed by The SCO Group and the ownership claims made. It is clear to me that while AT&T owned a good portion of several versions of System V, as a result of the incorporation of code from the CSRG and other sources, they never had full rights to all the source of any of the versions. Exactly what was conveyed from AT&T to USL, from USL to Novell, from Novell to the Santa Cruz Operation, and from the latter to Caldera (which became The SCO Group), may be adjudicated in one of the current suits.

The Daemon, the Gnu, and the Penguin

15 BTL after UNIX: Plan 9 and Inferno

In July 1990, I flew from Boston to London for the UKUUG Conference. (I was to give a talk on UNIX standards and specifications.) But there were three talks on the program that blew me away.

They concerned "Plan 9" a new OS being worked on at Bell Labs. It was named Plan 9 from Bell Labs after "Plan 9 from Outer Space," perhaps the worst science fiction movie ever filmed.

Plan 9 is a UNIX clone. But it presents a consistent interface which is easy to use. I am not going to go into it at any length. But, it was the successor to UNIX, which, Rob Pike said, was dead: "It's been dead for so long it doesn't even stink any more."

Rob delivered the keynote address at the UKUUG: "Plan 9 from Bell Labs." He's now at Google.

Dave Presotto then spoke about "Multiprocessor Streams for Plan 9." He's at Google, too.

Tom Duff talked about "Rc — A Shell for Plan 9 and UNIX Systems." Tom's now at Pixar, the proud owner of parts of several Oscars.

Fifteen years later, what had been the UNIX group (1127) has been dispersed. In addition to Rob, Dave and Tom,

- Ken Thompson joined Google in 2006.

- Brian Kernighan is a Professor at Princeton;

- Phil Winterbottom is CTO at Entrisphere;

- Howard Trickey is at Google;

- Gerard Holzmann is at NASA/JPL Laboratory for Reliable Software;

- Bob Flandrena is at Morgan Stanley;

- Sean Dorward is at Google;

- Doug McIlroy is teaching at Dartmouth.

Dennis Ritchie, with a few companions, remains at Lucent/BTL.

But, before it disappeared, the "1127 group" made yet another contribution to OS development: Inferno.

Inferno is a compact OS designed for building "cross-platform distributed systems." It can run on top of an existing OS, or as a stand-alone. The nomenclature owes much to Dave Presotto, who founded it firmly in Dante. The company marketing Inferno is Vita Nuova; the communications protocol is Styx; applications are written in type-safe Limbo, which has C-like syntax.

The 4th edition of Inferno was released in 2005 as free software, but under a mixture of licenses.

But 1127 is gone. In 2005 it was "reorganized" out of existence.[1]

---

[1]See my "going, Going, GONE," http://www.unixreview.com/articles/2005/0508/

16 Commercial UNIXes to BSDI

Well, I warned you that I wouldn't be bound by orderly chronology, as Spenser wrote historians are.

In the 15 years following the release of V6 (April 1976), Berkeley was not the only place where versions and clones of UNIX sprouted. While I doubt whether I can even enumerate all of them, the following will give an image of the geography of the field. To me, the most significant UNIX releases were:

- November 1976: Interactive Systems IS/1

- March 1978: 1BSD

- November 1978: Cromemco CROMIX

- November 1978: Technical Systems Consultants UniFLEX

- December 1978: V7

- April 1979: AT&T UNIX 32/V

- May 1979: 2BSD

- February 1980: 3BSD

- August 1980: MicroSoft XENIX OS

- September 1980: 4BSD

- 1980: Idris

- May 1981: 4.1BSD

- October 1981: System III

- November 1981: IBM CPIX

- November 1981: ULTRIX

- August 1982: 4.2BSD

- December 1982: AT&T System V

- March 1983: XENIX 3.0

- May 1983: Mark Williams Coherent

- September 1983: SCO Xenix

- March 1984: AT&T SVR2

- November 1984: SCO Xenix System V/286

- January 1985: BTL Eighth Edition

- November 1985: Apple A/UX

- November 1985: AT&T SVR3.0

- November 1985: AIX/RT 2

- November 1985: HP-UX 1.0

- May 1986: 4.3BSD

- August 1986: BTL Ninth Edition

- November 1986: MINIX 1.0

- November 1986: AT&T SVR3.2

- November 1986: HP-UX 1.2

- September 1987: SCO Xenix System V/386

- November 1987: NeXTStep

- November 1987: Acorn RISC UNIX

- January 1988: AIX 1.0

- May 1988: 4.3BSD-Tahoe

- October 1988: BSD Net/1

- September 1989: BTL Tenth Edition

- November 1989: Coherent 3.0

- November 1989: AT&T SVR4

- February 1990: SunOS 4.1

- October 1990: Solaris 1

- November 1990: Novell UNIXWare Personal Edition 1.1

- January 1991: Trusted Xenix 2.0

- May 1991: BSD Net/2

I've mentioned MINIX and the AT&T, BTL and BSD releases earlier. But several of the others are worth devoting a vignette to.

Interactive Systems

Interactive was founded by Peter Weiner in 1977. (Weiner had been Brian Kernighan's Ph.D. adviser at Princeton.) In 1978, Heinz Lycklama joined him in Santa Monica. Lycklama had just written LSX, a version of V6 UNIX for the LSI-11 microprocessor. Interactive's product was called IS/1 and ran on most PDP-11s. Interactive's UNIX was an important product for nearly a decade. In 1985, Interactive's IN/ix became the basis for AIX (announced 21 January 1986). Some of the later modifications to AIX were developed by Interactive under contract to IBM.

Cromix

Cromix was a proprietary UNIX clone of CROMEMCO. The CROMEMCO 100 ran on a Xilog 80 and had 512K of RAM, 50M of hard disk, and an XPU processor, enabling 32-bit processing. Founded in the early 1970s by Roger Melen and Harry Garland, Stanford students who lived in CROthers MEMorial Hall, it was incorporated in 1976. In 1985, it was bought up by Dynatech, and disappeared. But Cromix was the first UNIX clone. The CROMEMCO 100 and 300 ran both Cromix and System V. The 300 ran a 68000 timesliced with a Z80 coprocessor to enable multiuser CP/M WordStar.

TSC UniFLEX

Technical Systems Consultants wrote a driver for the then-new 5.25" drives in 1976: DOS MiniFLEX. It was superseded by FLEX for the 6800 a few months later. FLEX was adopted by virtually all of the 68xx SS-50-based computers. TSC now turned to producing a UNIX-like multi-user system for the 6809: UniFLEX. It was a failure.

MicroSoft XENIX

MicroSoft licensed 7th Edition from AT&T in 1979. On 25 August 1980 they announced that XENIX would be available for 16-bit processors (MicroSoft couldn't license the name, "UNIX"). XENIX wasn't identical to 7th Edition because MicroSoft incorporated several features from BSD.

MicroSoft didn't sell XENIX: it was licensed to manufacturers who were responsible for the porting. The first ports were to the Zilog Z8001, a 16-bit processor. Altos shipped one in early 1982. Tandy shipped one for 68000 systems in January 1983 and SCO released their port to the 8086 in September 1983. Though the license had been for V7, XENIX was based on System III.

XENIX 2.0

XENIX 2.0 (1985) was based on System V, and added support for 80286. However, MicroSoft apparently lost interest in XENIX after signing an agreement with IBM to develop OS/2. In 1987 MicroSoft transferred ownership of XENIX to SCO in exchange for 25% of the company. That same year, SCO ported Xenix to the 386 and Xenix 2.3.1 supported SCSI and TCP/IP.

Xenix became SCO UNIX in 1989.

Idris

P.J. (Bill) Plauger received his Ph.D. in Nuclear Physics from Michigan State in 1969. From 1969 to 1975 he was a Member of Technical Staff at Bell Labs. Together with Brian Kernighan, he wrote *Elements of Programming Style* (1974) and *Software Tools* (1976). He also writes science fiction, and won the 1975 John W. Campbell Award as the best new SF writer of 1975.

It was while writing *Software Tools* that Plauger left the Labs.

> I ended up leaving the Labs. I felt I didn't have a future there and that I'd better move on before they told me to move on [he told me]. And I was able to get a job at Yourdon ...

> After a few years of traveling all over the world lecturing, I felt that I wanted to get back to programming. Ed [Yourdon] had an opportunity to get a contract to do a commercial C compiler, and I talked him into doing it. I worked around the clock for a week ....

Plauger went on to form a three-man company, Whitesmiths.

> I think we started on August 1st, '78. We were going to sit down and write a C compiler from scratch — my third C compiler, I guess. I paid a lot of attention

to not having any notes from my Lab days or my Yourdon days .... I wrote like a fiend and by the end of November we had a compiler.

Whitesmiths' first compiler was for Fisher and Porter in Philadelphia. It was for the PDP-11. "We gave them an 8080 compiler by the middle of '79; a VAX compiler by the end of that year; and we gave them a 68000 compiler in the middle of 1980," he said. "And we were doing Idris at the same time." Idris was a UNIX-like multi-user multi-tasking operating system, written by Plauger and M. S. Krieger. Originally, Idris ran only on the PDP-11. But it was soon ported to the VAX, the 68000 and the 8086. In 1986, Atari hired Computer Tools International to port Idris to the Atari ST. Whitesmiths was sold to Intermetrics in 1988.

Mark Williams Coherent

The Coherent Operating System from Mark Williams was a UNIX-like OS for PCs. It was introduced in 1983. As I knew that several former University of Waterloo students had worked on it, I asked Tom Duff. Here it is, in his own words.

I was at Mark Williams from roughly August 1 to October 31 of 1980. After leaving the NYIT Graphics Lab, I had 6 months free (later reduced to 3 months) before I was scheduled to start at Lucasfilm. Mark Williams CEO Bob Swartz heard that I was available and asked if I'd like to work in Chicago for a while.

When I arrived, they had a working C compiler, assembler and loader and a version of ed, written by Dave Conroy, hosted on RSX.

Randall Howard was doing most of the kernel work. Johann George, David Levine and Bob Welland were also there, but I'm not sure what they were working on — Johann was probably doing kernel stuff.

Dave Conroy, Randall, Johann and I were all friends
at Waterloo in the early '70s. This was an amazing
crew: Dave Conroy most recently was in charge of
engineering the Mac Mini, Randall founded MKS,
Johann founded Sourcelight Technologies (Randall
and Johann are both semi-retired VCs now), David
Levine wrote a legendary early video game called
Ballblazer, and Bob worked on the design of a bunch
of important Amiga hardware.

When I arrived, it was pretty clear that the kernel
was pretty much taken care of (though it wouldn't
be running well enough for daily use until after I'd
left), but nobody was working on user-space stuff.
So I opened the 6th edition manual to page one
and started implementing commands. In the three
months that I was there, I think I did A through M.
As I remember, I started at make, then jumped back
to ar and just plowed through. I remember make,
diff and dc being a lot of fun.

And I did units, because the library research required
to dig up the more obscure quantities seemed interesting.

While I was there, Ciaran O'Donnell (another friend
from Waterloo) visited for two weeks during which
he wrote, in a feat of coding acrobatics such as I have
never seen before or since, a complete, functioning
YACC clone, working just from Aho and Johnson's
1974 *Computing Surveys* paper.

Coherent eventually ran on most 286, 386 and 486 boxes. It
actually had support for X11 Windows. The Mark Williams
Company went bankrupt in 1995.

A/UX

A/UX was Apple's entry to the world of UNIX in 1988. It was based on SVR2.2 with elements of SVR3 and SVR4 as well as some 4.2BSD and 4.3BSD. It is POSIX and SVID compliant. From A/UX v2 on, it included TCP/IP. The last version (3.1.1) was released in 1995.

NeXTSTEP

A UNIX-like kernel based on Mach (CMU) with many BSD features and display PostScript with a windowing engine lay at the heart of NeXTSTEP. Previewed several times beginning in 1986, it was eventually released on 18 September 1989. Though it featured a microkernel, it succumbed. The last release (3.3) came out in early 1995.

There are, of course, many other UNIX-like things one could talk about, but I never found Trusted Xenix nor the RISC version nor Compaq's NonStop-UX very interesting.

17 The Hurd and BSDI

The Hurd

Richard Stallman had long wanted a GNU replacement for the UNIX kernel. A first pass, Trix, barely got going in the late 1980s. This changed, however, when Thomas Bushnell came to Boston and joined the GNU effort.

Thomas was born in Albuquerque, N.Mex. He attended Carnegie-Mellon University for a year (1985–86), the University of New Mexico for nearly two years, worked, enrolled at the University of Massachusetts Boston, and received a B.A. *summa cum laude* in 1999 in philosophy and classics. Thomas is a brother in the Brotherhood of St. Gregory, an Episcopal order. He received his M.A. in Philosophy from the University of California, Irvine, in 2003 and is currently a Ph.D. candidate there.

Thomas worked as an Assistant Systems Administrator at UNM from 1986–89 and for the FSF from 1990–1998. He told me:

> I wrote a BASIC interpreter as a demonstration that I could code before I was hired, since my most interesting work before then was on the then-proprietary UNIX kernel. My interpreter had a feature that would let you dynamically load math functions out of the C library — before shared libraries existed. I worked on GNU tar as well, before my main work was the Hurd.

The GNU Hurd is the GNU project's replacement for the UNIX kernel. The Hurd is a collection of servers that run on the Mach microkernel to implement file systems, network protocols, file access control, and other features that are implemented by the UNIX kernel or similar kernels (such as Linux). Thomas told me:

> RMS was a very strong believer — wrongly, I think — in a very greedy-algorithm approach to code reuse issues. My first choice was to take the BSD 4.4-Lite release and make a kernel. I knew the code, I knew how to do it. It is now perfectly obvious to me that this would have succeeded splendidly and the world would be a very different place today.
>
> RMS wanted to work together with people from Berkeley on such an effort. Some of them were interested, but some seem to have been deliberately dragging their feet: and the reason now seems to be that they had the goal of spinning off BSDI. A GNU based on 4.4-Lite would undercut BSDI.
>
> So RMS said to himself, "Mach is a working kernel, 4.4-Lite is only partial, we will go with Mach." It was a decision which I strongly opposed. But ultimately it was not my decision to make, and I made the best go I could at working with Mach and doing something new from that standpoint.
>
> This was all way before Linux; we're talking 1991 or so.

Currently, the Hurd runs on IA32 machines. The Hurd should, and probably will, eventually be ported to other hardware architectures or other microkernels in the future.

According to Thomas:

> `Hurd' stands for `Hird of UNIX-Replacing Daemons'. And, then, `Hird' stands for `Hurd of Interfaces Representing Depth'. We have here, to my knowledge, the first software to be named by a pair of mutually recursive acronyms.

The FSF states: "The Hurd, together with the GNU Mach microkernel, the GNU C Library and the other GNU and non-GNU programs in the GNU system, provide a rather complete and usable operating system today. It is not ready for production use, as there are still many bugs and missing features. However, it should be a good base for further development and non-critical application usage."

Unfortunately, the Hurd is late. By 1995, Linux had many users. By 2000, it was a well-understood and popular system. By 2005, Linux had millions of users and the support of IBM. It was seen as a threat by Microsoft. The Hurd, unfortunately, is still "not ready for production use."

BSDI

Beginning in 1989, 386BSD was a port of 4BSD to the x86 architecture by Bill and Lynne Jolitz. The first public release was version 0.0 in March 1991. They documented their "Porting Unix to the 386" work and code in a series of widely-read magazine articles and an excellent book "The Basic Kernel Source Code Secrets," Vol. 1 (1996) ISBN 1-57398-026-9. 386BSD code was used in 4.3BSD NET/2, BSDI's BSD/386, NetBSD, and FreeBSD.

BSDI was the first company to offer a full version of BSD UNIX for the Intel platform.

Despite the fact that everything was in the public eye and exposed at the USL vs. BSDI trial, there appears to be confusion as to the history of BSDI.

I think ThomasindexBushnell, Thomas was right, to a certain extent.

While several Berkeley developers were involved in the formation of BSDI in 1990 91, none left the University of California to join Berkeley Software Design, Inc. at the outset. BSDI was founded by Rick Adams, who told me:

It was my idea and my funding. I also handled the

logistics (via UUNET) and the little matter of the lawsuit.

Donn Seeley related:

> The first organizational meeting occurred at a bar in Boulder during the Boulder Berkeley Workshop in October 1990. I was invited to the meeting without any advance warning and to my surprise, I was offered a job. My recollection is that Rick, Mike, Kirk, Keith, and Bill J[olitz] were present at the meeting. I believe that a more formal meeting was held in early December 1990 at Kirk's house [in Berkeley], where we voted to go ahead with the proposal. I think this meeting was when we came up with the name BSDI.

> We decided to work under UUNET's wing for a while so that we would not alert any potential competition; that continued until the summer of 1991. I was to start work as soon as possible; I took an extended vacation from my job at the University of Utah, and set up shop in my parents' basement in Bellingham, WA, with a PC provided by Rick, running mt Xinu Mach/BSD (I think). (I don't remember exactly when I gave notice at Utah, but I set things up so that my employment terminated shortly before the Winter USENIX [21–25 January 1991; Dallas].) I couldn't actually work directly on the OS, since it still contained licensed code at that point.

> The BSD distribution was still hung up on the issue of certain possibly licensed files, so my job was to work on freely available software. I started with the compiler toolchain (based on GCC 1). Once it was clear that there would be missing files, I went ahead and wrote a replacement for the Berkeley init(8) program. I'm not sure whether Bill was working on

BSDI-related stuff at this point, but I'm pretty sure that he had started by the time of the 1991 Winter USENIX, where we all met again.

At that time Kirk McKusick was President of USENIX, Rick was in Dallas to report on UUNET and recruit, Trent Hein was chairing the session on File Systems, and Keith Bostic and Mike Karels were part of the CSRG. It wasn't hard to call a meeting.

Trent was a student at the University of Colorado, where he was a co-author (with Evi Nemeth et al.) of both the UNIX and the Linux system administration handbooks. He worked on the 4.4BSD port to the MIPS architecture. More recently, he was co-founder of Applied Trust Engineering. He said:

> I can concretely say that the original engineering team "hired" by BSDI (Spring, 1991) consisted of Donn Seeley, Bill Jolitz and myself. Bill left BSDI later that year. Rob Kolstad joined the BSDI team much later. [Kolstad was Secretary of USENIX at that time.]

Mike Karels told me:

> I'd say that the founders were Rick Adams, Keith Bostic, Kirk McKusick, me, Bill Jolitz, and Donn Seeley, in approximately that historical order. This group was involved at the time of formation. Bill and Donn were the first two full-time employees, and Trent started about the same time at just less than full-time. They worked for UUNET temporarily until the company started operations, which I think was about July 1991. Bill left at the end of November '91, and Rob [Kolstad] started December 1. The proximity of the dates is not a coincidence. I started February 1, 1992, at which time two Russians had also started, and also Jeff Polk. My departure from Berkeley and

position at BSDI were announced at USENIX in January '92 [San Francisco], at which Bill made a famous appearance.

I asked Rick to clarify and he affirmed:

The first employees were Donn Seeley and Bill Jolitz. Peter Collinson signed on very early for European sales and Bob Kummerfeld for Australia.

We picked up Vadim Antonov and Igor Belchinsky from the USSR that fall (1991). Rob Kolstad came on as president in December 1991.

Donn Seeley provided yet more detail.

Bill believed that he deserved a larger role as systems architect, press contact and marketer. His coding contributions mainly came before he started working for UUNET/BSDI, by porting to PCs the drivers we'd written at Utah for HP 68k systems, and writing the locore assembly source and related files. As for Bill's departure, the straw that broke the camel's back was an issue with Bill's unauthorized expenses for a trip to Europe, if I recall correctly, but it was clear long before this point that Bill was not happy. Rick was BSDI's original president, but he was asked to separate UUNET from BSDI by UUNET's first big investors, so he enlisted Rob to replace him.

Insofar as Keith Bostic was concerned, he said:

I joined much later than Mike and the founders, though. I stayed at UC Berkeley for quite some time after BSDI was founded.

Another person mentioned by Rick was Peter Collinson. In 1980–81, Collinson (then at the University of Kent in Canterbury) was offered a Usenet feed by Teus Hagen at the CWI in Amsterdam. They couldn't dial out, but the CWI would dial in, via a modem brought into the UK by Martin Levy. In April 1982, he was instrumental in the formation of EUnet.

"I think it was the Fall of 1993 that Rick asked me to sell things in Europe," Collinson told me.

> The earliest date on a file that I have is September 1993. I think I was at a BSDI meeting at the USENIX conference in San Francisco in January 1994 [January 21–24].

> When did I leave? — we were forced out by the sales department at the end of 1995 — we had the fax in September — we settled and were gone by January 1996.

> We in Europe did OK — but we were not that good at Sales — and would have had to think hard about Sales-led sales rather than Techy-led sales very soon anyway.

In 2000, BSDI merged with Walnut Creek CDROM and then with Telenet Systems. The next year, Wind River Systems purchased the software business. Renaming itself iXsystems with plans to specialize in hardware, the server business was acquired by Offmyserver in 2002. I asked Collinson why he thought BSDI had failed.

> BSDI didn't really fail. It allowed Linux to flourish unhindered by lawsuits; but it was not really technically viable. BSDI couldn't move quickly enough to keep up with the technical changes — and Linux could because of the customer base which was a new generation of UNIX hackers and lovers.

The Daemon, the Gnu, and the Penguin

18 The BSDs

It is one thing to talk of the development of BSDI from Net/1 and Net/2. Another branch growing out of the CSRG at Berkeley is that of NetBSD, FreeBSD and OpenBSD.

NetBSD is a freely redistributable, open source version of BSD. It was the second open source BSD descendant to be formally released, after 386BSD, and continues to be actively developed. Noted for its portability and quality of design and implementation, it is often used in embedded systems and as a starting point for porting to new computer architectures.

Like FreeBSD, NetBSD was derived from 4.3BSD via the Net/2 and 386BSD. The project began as a result of frustration within the 386BSD community with the pace and direction of the operating system's development. The four founders of the NetBSD project, Chris Demetriou, Theo de Raadt, Adam Glass and Charles Hannum, felt that a more open model would be beneficial; a model centered on portable, clean, correct code. Their goal was to achieve a unified, multi-platform, production-quality, BSD-based operating system.

Because of the importance of networks, de Raadt suggested the name "NetBSD," which was readily accepted by the others.

The NetBSD source code repository was established on March 21, 1993 and the first official release, NetBSD 0.8, was in April, 1993. In August of the same year, NetBSD 0.9 was released, with many enhancements and bug fixes. This was still a PC-platform-only, although work was underway to add support for other architectures.

NetBSD 1.0 was released in October, 1994. This was the first multi-platform release, supporting the PC, HP 9000 Series 300,

Amiga, 68k Macintosh, Sun-4c series and the PC532. Also in this release, legally encumbered Net/2-derived source code was replaced with equivalent code from 4.4BSD-Lite, per the USL v BSDI settlement.

In 1994, for disputed reasons, one of the founders, Theo de Raadt, was forced out of the project. He later founded a new project, OpenBSD, from a forked version of NetBSD 1.0 near the end of 1995.

The current release of NetBSD is version 4.0 (December 19, 2007).

FreeBSD is a free operating system descended from AT&T UNIX via BSD, through 386BSD and 4.4BSD. It runs on Intel x86 family PC compatible computers, DEC Alpha, Sun UltraSPARC, IA-64, AMD64, PowerPC, ARM, and NEC PC-98 architectures as well as the Microsoft Xbox.

FreeBSD's development began in 1993 with a quickly growing, unofficial patchkit maintained by users of the 386BSD operating system. This patchkit forked from 386BSD and grew into an operating system taken from 4.3BSD-Lite (Net/2) tape with many 386BSD components and code from the FSF. The first official release was FreeBSD 1.0 in December 1993, coordinated by Jordan Hubbard, Nate Williams and Rod Grimes with a name thought up by David Greenman. Walnut Creek CDROM agreed to distribute FreeBSD on CD and gave the project a machine to work on along with a fast Internet connection, which Hubbard later said helped stir FreeBSD's rapid growth. A "highly successful" FreeBSD 1.1 release followed in May 1994.

However, there were legal concerns about the BSD Net/2 release source code used in 386BSD, so the FreeBSD project re-engineered most of the system using 4.4BSD-Lite, which had none of the AT&T source code earlier BSD versions had depended upon, making it an unbootable operating system. After a lot of work, the code was released as FreeBSD 2.0 in January 1995.

FreeBSD 2.0 featured a revamp of the original Mach virtual

memory system, which was optimized for performance under high loads. This release also introduced the FreeBSD Ports system, which made downloading, building and installing third party software quite easy. By 1996 FreeBSD had become popular among commercial and ISP (Internet Service Provider) users, powering extremely successful sites like Walnut Creek CDROM, Yahoo! and Hotmail.

The Trusted BSD project provides a set of trusted operating system extensions to FreeBSD. It was begun primarily by Robert Watson with the goal of implementing concepts from the Common Criteria for Information Technology Security Evaluation and the Orange Book. (The "Orange Book" is the US Department of Defense Standard *Trusted Computer System Evaluation Criteria* [December 1985], frequently referred to by the color of its cover or as TCSEC.) This project is ongoing and many of its extensions have been integrated into FreeBSD.

The main focuses of the TrustedBSD project are access control lists (ACLs), security event auditing, extended file system attributes, fine-grained capabilities and mandatory access controls (MAC). The project has also ported the NSA's FLASK/TE from SELinux to FreeBSD. Other work includes the development of OpenBSM, an open source implementation of Sun's Basic Security Module API and audit log file format, which supports an extensive security audit system. This was shipped as part of FreeBSD 6.2. Other infrastructure work in FreeBSD came about as part of the TrustedBSD Project.

While most components of the TrustedBSD project were eventually folded into the main sources for FreeBSD, many features, once fully matured, have found their way into other operating systems. For example, OpenPAM and UFS2 have been adopted by NetBSD. Moreover, the TrustedBSD MAC Framework and TrustedBSD Audit implementation have been adopted by Apple Computer for Mac OS X.

Much of this work was sponsored by DARPA.

The Daemon, the Gnu, and the Penguin

The current release of FreeBSD is version 7.0 (February 27, 2008).

Starting in the summer of 1996, OpenBSD developers began frequently auditing their source code for misuse of various standard programming functions and basic software bugs — resulting in fixing numerous real and potential security holes. They also implemented and invented various security technologies. OpenBSD's stated goal is to be number one in the industry for security and their website currently reads "Only two remote holes in the default install, in more than 10 years!"

The current release of OpenBSD is version 4.2 (November 1, 2007).

Much more could be written, but the really important thing to me is the continued viability of the Berkeley UNIX streams within the envelope of free software.

Excursus: The GPL and Other Licenses

A license is formal permission for something. In general, this is written permission. Historically, such things began with (un-written) permission to "go upon or use the land of another" – to cross a lord's manor or forest, for example — as a "personal privilege, not constituting an interest in the land." That is, the recipient was allowed to do something, but this did not entail any ownership rights.

Copyright is a form of license. It is a license granted by the state to the "author." The first copyright statute was the Statute of Anne, usually cited as 1709. (As with almost everything, the date is ambiguous: the Statute was introduced in 1709, but "passed into law" on 10 April 1710. The actual publication of the Act (BL 8 Anne c. 19, 261) is just headed "Anno Octavo." But, as the eighth year of Anne's reign terminated on 17 March 1710, contemporaries must have thought of the statute as dating from 1709. On the other hand, Adam Budd (*TLS* 15 July 2005, p. 24) calls it "The Copyright Act of 1710.")

At any rate, the Statute required booksellers to record their titles in the Stationer's Register to gain protection for their "literary property." All registrations stem from this.[1]

In addition to copyright, the law recognizes patents and trade secrets (as well as trademarks and "trade dress"), insofar as intellectual property rights are concerned. Until a few years ago, it was generally held that patents needed to be capable of

---

[1] Anyone interested in the history should read Ronan Deazley's *On the Origin of the Right to Copy* (Oxford, 2004).

physical instantiation. In 1997, patents on "business methods" were recognized. The next year, Amazon.com filed for a patent on "one-click" purchasing. In 2008, the battle over software patents is still being fought. I'm certain that it will continue for years.

There is no formal filing where trade secrets are concerned, and most suits have concerned improprieties: breach of contract and outright theft, for example. Attempting to keep the knowledge secret (think of the famed Coca-Cola recipe) is basic here.

To all effects and purposes, software licensing began when UNIX was ported to the Interdata 7 (in Australia) and the Interdata 8 (at BTL). Prior to that, an OS ran only on the machine with which it was sold or, in the case of UNIX, on the PDP-11. (And, if you were running UNIX and had the misfortune to call DEC service, they would tell you they "didn't know" about the alien system.)

The first "open source" license was that of the University of California at Berkeley (I will not distinguish between "free" and "open" source at this time). It came about through an active belief in academic freedom — the right to examine and investigate.

As has been related earlier, the specific impetus given to Stallman to write the original version of the GPL was the refusal of LISP Machines to share their code.

Though there are now over 50 variants on the Berkeley Software License and the GPL, all free and open licenses trace their roots to these two. And, actually, I see both of these as having a common origin in "the right to tinker."

My guess is that there is no one reading this whose childhood is not littered with the parts of alarm clocks, toy trains, toasters, robots, radios, etc. (Yes, there is always an extra screw, or gear or spring.) Part of learning how things work is taking them apart and reassembling them (or attempting to). Breaking them. Part of learning is destructive analysis.

And that tinkering leads to improvements.

Both the BSL (Berkeley Software License) and the GPL are founded in the notion that opening source code to examination leads to extensions and improvements that can subsequently be reincorporated into future code.

But proprietary software vendors (and hardware manufacturers) don't permit that.

In fact, as Professor Edward Felten has repeatedly pointed out, the Digital Millennium Copyright Act (DMCA), specifically criminalizes tinkering. It also criminalizes, for example, access to no-longer-current Web pages (The Wayback Machine was sued by Healthcare Advocates for retaining archived pages to be recalled: *New York Times* 13 July 2005. While the courts may dismiss the suit, its very presence chills debate.).

By and large, legislative bodies are staffed by individuals well below the genius level in IQ. The result is (all too frequently) that they are manipulated by others into enacting laws that are far from perfect. In Sergei Prokofiev's "Peter and the Wolf," the wolf, in his haste, swallowed the duck whole. In their headlong run to "protect" everything, the US Congress added DMCA Title V, sections 1301–1332, to protect "Vessel Hull Designs." Formerly, because, hulls are "useful articles whose form cannot be clearly separated from their function," their design was not protected under copyright law. Such design now is.

To take a bad law to its extreme, the letter of the DMCA would appear to make, for example, tinkering with the mechanism on a child's bank (if a key is lost or mislaid) criminal, for it does not distinguish among "security devices" (though, in general, the DMCA does specify copyright matters).

While the evils of the large media-producing companies are many, this "slop-over" into other areas was, I'm sure, unintentional. However, the DMCA in the US (the parallel has not yet been enacted in Canada, though it has been tabled in Parliament), and its support by WIPO, are truly stultifying where research and development are concerned.

For details on the run of licenses, see Lawrence Rosen's superb book.[2] However, I'd like to mention some things I believe make a few licenses beyond the GPL and Berkeley important. (A large number of licenses may be found on opensource.org.)

- The MIT derivative includes a "right to sublicense" extension.

- The Apache license is the only "major open source derivative of the academic license" to "protect the Apache trademark."

- Mozilla transforms the GPL by incorporating "files containing derivative works," not merely "derivative works."

- The Open Group now has a "Test license."

- The W3C has a "Patent License."

"Free as in freedom."

---

[2]*Open Source Licensing* (Prentice Hall PTR, 2005).

19 Finding Stuff in the Attic

Before we travel much further, let's look at the spread of the Internet.

The ARPANET became functional in 1969: at the end of that year, there were four nodes. In January 1976, there were 63 (so much for 5- or 6-bit addressing). Five years later, in August 1981, Host Table #152 listed 213 hosts. In May 1982, Host Table #166 listed 235.

The great switch in addressing to the domain system occurred on January 1, 1983. It was none too soon. The 562 hosts of August 1983 just wouldn't have been feasible under the older protocols and the older scheme.[1]

Here's the growth over the next few years:

Date	Hosts
10/84	1024
10/85	1961
02/86	2308
11/86	5089
12/87	28174
07/88	33000
10/88	56000
01/89	80000
10/89	159000
10/90	313000
10/91	617000

---

[1]There is a more extensive history of Internet addressing in my *Big Book of IPv6 Addressing RFCs* (Morgan Kaufman, 2000).

I'll stop there for a while, for several reasons, not least because this marks the advent of both the Web and of Linux. But because the time denotes other things as well.

On the political front, the US Department of Defense relaxed its notion that only government, academic and research sites could connect. This was partially the result of recognizing the expansion of private networks (like IBM's VNet and Prodigy) and of networks distributing news and mail (UUNET, Bitnet, Fidonet), as well as the recognition that the network of networks was already vastly larger than just the US and its "allies."

On the "engineering" side, the advent of the desktop machine and the commercial modem, meant that individuals could have a computer at home and plug in to their telephone lines. All for under $3000!

In 1971, BBN estimated 10 users per host. It was extrapolating from 617000 to one million and multiplying by BBN's estimate that gave the Internet Society the 10,000,000 users that *TIME* magazine claimed in 1992. In an informal poll a decade ago, I found that I knew individuals who owned a dozen domains and who were sole user on most (0.1 user/domain?) and that IBM's T.J. Watson Research Center had over 4000 users and one domain. I didn't know then and don't know now what the "correct" ratio is. Craig Partridge estimated 5/domain in 1994. John Quarterman estimated 3.5.

These sound more reasonable than double or triple those ratios.

The advent of NAT (Network Address Translation) makes all the ratios and estimates yet more unreliable: we have no way of determining in any accurate fashion how many desktops on a LAN are lurking behind a single address, any more than knowing how many telephone numbers are assigned to a building enables you to know how many instruments are connected to each number.

But in 2003 (the last dates for which the numbers seem feasible), there were about 175 million domains. Using the growth

Chapter 19. Finding Stuff in the Attic

rates of 1995–2002 for 2002–2006 would mean 600–700 million domains at the end of 2006, and about 2,000,000,000 users worldwide. (This counts students in schools and people in libraries, of course.) Just under a third of the world's population has access to an Internet-connected device. By 2008 that might be just about half. In January 1970, there had been about two dozen. But many machines and many users means lots and lots of stuff: raw data, text, statistics, etc. And, unless your friend in Corner Brook, Newfoundland, lets you know that she has put all of Donne's verses and Vondel's plays in various files, you'll never be able to find them, even though ftp (the file transfer protocol) might enable you to download them.

Library catalogs are designed to enable users to locate the books they are looking for. There are master lists of serials (magazines, newspapers, journals, etc.) so that one can find out which libraries subscribe to which magazines. But what about the bits, as opposed to the pages?

In 1990, when there were about 300,000 hosts, three students at McGill University in Montreal set about writing a search engine that would poll FTP archives on a regular basis. Alan Emtage, Bill Heelan and Peter Deutsch called it Archie. Soon there were other search engines, too: Gopher, Jughead, Veronica, WAIS (Wide Area Information Server).

Gopher was a system for organizing and displaying files found on Internet servers. It was very useful, for a brief period of time. The University of Minnesota, where Gopher was developed, wanted to profit from it. Tim Berners-Lee offered the Web program free. Though he's now Sir Timothy, he's not a millionaire. But, by 1994, the World Wide Web had swept away all the other browsers.

Why is this important? Well, in 1973, when Dennis M. Ritchie and Ken Thompson gave that first UNIX paper, there were about 200 people in the room. There were just over 40 hosts on the Net. Even at that 10-users-per host number, that would have meant only double the number actually at the presentation.

107

The Daemon, the Gnu, and the Penguin

Word of mouth and then the *CACM* paper were how the word got out. When Linus Torvalds posted his note on the comp.os.minix newsgroup, there were about 200 groups. There were over 600,000 hosts connected to the Internet. The potential audience for Linux was enormous. And transmission was virtually instantaneous.

I wonder what my long–ago Toronto colleague, Marshall McLuhan, would say; today's Internet and Web are "hot" media far beyond his notions.

The real changes that have come about are directly tied to speed of communication: in the seventeenth and eighteenth centuries, communicative speed was that of the horse or the stagecoach or the packet boat. Then, in the mid-19th century, Morse invented the telegraph (demonstrated in early 1838); less than 50 years later, Bell's telephone was a real success.

But Bell knew that no one would ever want a telephone in their home. I'm certain that the cellphone in one's pocket would have been truly unimaginable.

But speed of communication was vital to the growth of mercantilism, too. In 1815 the Rothschilds made a fortune by manipulating information as to the outcome of the Battle of Waterloo.

20 The Web

Just what will inspire invention is infinitely variable.

Ted Nelson says that his notion of hypertext was inspired by Vannevar Bush's "As We May Think," which was first published in *The Atlantic* in January 1945, and by S.T. Coleridge's poem "Kubla Khan" (1798, published in 1816).

Sir Timothy John Berners-Lee says that in his childhood home there was a book entitled *Enquire Within upon Everything*, a "musty old book of Victorian advice." What we now think of as the Web, was originally called "Enquire."[1]

The son of two mathematicians, Tim Berners-Lee took a degree in physics from Queens College Oxford and then worked for Plessey Telecommunications and D.G. Nash, prior to going to CERN[2] as an independent contractor in 1980.

At CERN, Berners-Lee felt a need for researchers to locate and share information. Having read Nelson's work, he determined that hypertext was the appropriate model to use. With the aid of Robert Cailliau, he set out to build a prototype system — Enquire. But Berners-Lee left CERN at the end of 1980 to work for Image Computing Systems.

In 1984, Berners-Lee returned to CERN as a fellow and immediately went to work on CERN's Internet site, which by 1989 was the largest single site in Europe. He jumped at the opportunity of "marrying" the notion of hypertext and the Internet.

---

[1] *Enquire Within . . .* was one of the very many Victorian compendia. It was originally published in 1859 and went through over 100 printings and editions, the most recent of which was published in New York in 1978.

[2] Organisation Europeenne pour la Recherche Nucleaire, on the border between France and Geneva

In Chapter 6 , I outlined Lesk's development of uucp (1976) and the evolution of Netnews and the ftp search engines (Gopher, Archie, WAIS). What Berners-Lee was creating was the logical product of this decade's work by a variety of people.

"I just had to take the hypertext idea and connect it to the TCP and DNS ideas and — ta-da! — the World Wide Web." [3] Berners-Lee envisaged knowledge as an immense reticulum, and so he named his creation the World Wide Web. To navigate within the Web, he designed and built the first browser (WorldWideWeb) and developed it on NextStep. The first server was called httpd (hyper text transfer protocol daemon). The new proposal for this was written on November 12, 1990; work was begun the next day. The tools were written over Christmas holiday 1990–91. The world learned about it on August 6, 1991, when Berners-Lee posted a summary of his project on the newsgroup alt.hypertext. Think of it: the Web was announced on Usenet!

The Web is an information space in which items of interest ("resources") are tagged with global identifiers (Uniform Resource Identifiers [URIs]). The Web is not the Internet, it is a service operating on the Internet.

And on April 3, 1993, CERN announced that the code would be free, with no fee. This last was crucial, for the University of Minnesota had succeeded in dashing the enthusiasm for Gopher through the cold water of a fee.

The Internet was free.

TCP/IP was free.

UUCP was free.

Gopher had no chance.

The World Wide Web now did.

I'm certain that Vannevar Bush had no notion of the inspiration his 1945 article would provide: to Doug Englebart and Ted Nelson; to Tim Berners-Lee; to innumerable others. But what has

[3]For a truly personal view of this history, see Berners-Lee, *Weaving the Web* (1999).

been salient over these 60 years has been the notion of building on the previous constructs, which have been freely accessible.

Hypertext (in the sense most of us use it) has little to do with what Nelson wrote about in the late 1960s and the 1970s. I asked about the Web: "Berners-Lee came to my office in 1992 and showed me what he'd done," he told me. "I was polite, didn't say I thought it was stupid, and took him to lunch. That was the extent of our interaction."

Ted continued: "The web has nothing whatsoever to do with my notion of hypertext, and I am still fighting for what I believe in. Real Soon Now, I hope this month, I'll be announcing a new spec called Transliterature. Watch for it. "What would I have to do with http?"[4]

But hypertext was Nelson's concept. It has been refashioned into something very different.

And I can't even buy a bar of soap that doesn't have a URL on it.

---

[4]See www.transliterature.org for the current status of Nelson's work.

The Daemon, the Gnu, and the Penguin

21 Just for Fun

I frequently point to August 1969 as the "birthmonth" of UNIX. A few days later, the ARPANET (soon to become the Internet) was born. And, on 28 December 1969, Linus Torvalds was born.

- Murray Hill, N.J.

- Los Angeles, Calif.

- Helsinki, Finland

Where Free Software is concerned, the geographical spread is equally interesting:

- Richard Stallman, New York and Cambridge, Mass.

- Tim Berners-Lee, Oxford, UK, and Geneva, Switzerland

- Linus Torvalds, Helsinki, Finland, and now Portland, Oreg.

Linus was born into the Swedish minority of Finland (about 5% of the 5,000,000 Finns). Linus was a "math guy" throughout his schooling. Early on, he "inherited" a Commodore VIC-20 (released in June 1980) from his grandfather; in 1987 he spent his savings on a Sinclair QL (released in January 1984, the "Quantum Leap," with a Motorola 68008 running at 7.5Hz and 128kB of RAM, was intended for the small business and the serious hobbyist). It ran Q-DOS. And it was what got Linus involved.

> One of the things I hated about the QL was that it had a read-only operating system. You couldn't change things ...

> [I] bought a new assembler ... and an editor ... Both...
> worked fine, but they were on the microdrives and
> couldn't be put on the EEPROM. So I wrote my
> own editor and assembler and used *them* for all my
> programming. Both were written in assembly lan-
> guage, which is incredibly stupid by today's stan-
> dards ... (*Just for Fun*, 2001, p. 45).

That was the beginning. A high school student, interested
in bettering his system, wrote the tools he wanted. During
his first year at the University, Linus tells us that he did little
programming, and at the end of that year, he enlisted in the
Finnish army to fulfill his obligation. He was 19. He "got out"
on 7 May 1990.

In the fall of 1990, the University of Helsinki installed its first
UNIX machine, a MicroVAX running Ultrix. But, Linus was
"eager to work with UNIX by experimenting with what I was
learning in Andrew Tanenbaum's book" (p. 53).

Linus read all 700-odd pages of *Operating Systems*. The book
"lived on my bed." One of the things that struck Linus about
UNIX was its openness. Another was its simplicity. And then
came a bolt from the blue: in early 1991, Lars Wirzenius dragged
Linus to the Polytechnic University of Helsinki to hear Richard
Stallman. "I don't remember much about the talk," Linus says.
"But I guess something from his speech must have sunk in. After
all, I later ended up using the GPL for Linux."

But on 5 January 1991, Linus had gotten his father to drive
him to a "mom and pop" computer store, where he had ordered
a no-name 4-meg, 33MHz, 386 box, so he could get it home. He
was now 21. The box came with DOS, but Linus wanted MINIX,
and ordered it. It took a month to find its way to Finland. But
it arrived. And Linus fed the 16 diskettes to the machine. And
then he began "playing" with it. The first thing he wrote was a
terminal emulator: "That's how Linux got started. With my test
programs turning into a terminal emulator."

Tinkering.
Because Linus was truly dependent upon the Internet and
(specifically) the comp.os.minix newsgroup, we can date events
far more accurately than we could have in earlier decades.
We know that Linus' first posting to comp.os.minix, asking
about the POSIX standard, was 3 July 1991. And we can see
his posting about "doing a (free) operating system (just a hobby,
won't be big and professional like gnu) ... This has been brewing
since April ... ," of 25 August 1991.
There was a reasonable expression of interest. We thus know
that Linus put what we would now call Linux 0.01 up on the
University of Helsinki ftp site on 17 September 1991. "No more
than one or two people ever checked it out," he said.
The following January there was discernible growth in the
Linux community, leading (I think) to the attack on Linux by
Andy Tanenbaum on 29 January 1992. Perhaps more important,
in the spring Orest Zborowsky ported the X Window System to
Linux.
The number of Linux users continued to grow, as did the
versions of the software. .01 was 63KB compressed. Only a few
weeks later, Linus posted .02 on 5 October. On 19 December, v.11
was posted; and on 5 January 1992, v.12 — 108KB compressed —
appeared. On 7 March, there was v.95 and on 25 May 1992, v.96,
with support for X, and taking up 174KB compressed.
It was barely a year since Linus' first posting, but in 1992 SuSE
was formed, in February Bruce Perens released MCC Linux, and
on 8 December, Yggdrasil alpha was released. Free OS software
was now truly available. On both sides of the Atlantic. And
there was more to come.
1993 began with Yggdrasil's beta release (18 February) and
went on to Red Hat's being set up by Marc Ewing. August 1993
brought us Debian (from Debbie and Ian Murdock).
And, on 5 November 1993, Linus travelled to Amsterdam
and spoke at the NLUUG (Netherlands UNIX Users' Group)
meeting.

On 12 March 1994, Linus released Linux 1.0, basically v0.99, patch level 157. It was the first stable kernel distribution. I don't want to go into extensive detail here. But I think that there are a number of important points to be made:

- The birth, growth and development was totally unorganized.

- It was well-distributed, geographically.

- It was conducted via the Internet.

Ted Ts'o was one of the first Linux users in the US. I spoke to him over dinner in Atlanta.

> I was working as an undergraduate staff person at MIT — I was planning to go to graduate school, but I got caught up in projects. So I've got some courses, but no grad degree.
>
> Kerberos was in wide use at MIT by 1987 (it was invented by Cliff Neumann, Jerry Saltzer, and Jeff Schiller). I didn't start work on Kerberos until about 1992 or so, when John Kohl stepped down as the team lead to go to graduate school. My three years at Project Athena was as a student systems programmer, working on the BSD 4.3 kernel and a variety of various system utilities for Project Athena, from 1987 until I graduated in 1990, and during that time I worked for Dan Geer. After I graduated, I started at the MIT Network Operations group, where I reported to Jeff Schiller. During the summer of 1991, I was asked to put together a help desk application written using Ingres as the backend database, and curses as the text-based interface. This was a nightmare of a project, with constantly changing requirements and ultimately turned into a death march before the plug was finally mercifully pulled on it sometime in the fall of 1991.

It was in the midst of this that I discovered Linux,
and it was at least partially responsible for preserv-
ing my sanity, since it allowed me to get back to
doing systems programming instead of dealing with
clueless users who kept on jerking me around on
what they wanted out of this help desk application.
I came across Linux on Usenet. I think it was .08 or
.09 that had been cross-posted.

Ted later went to work for Red Hat, and from there to IBM.
The important thing here is that thanks to the Internet and to
Usenet, the work of a hobbyist in Finland could be picked up
elsewhere in Europe, in Australia, and in the US.

"There was fairly strong social cohesion," Ted told me. "Linux
was the first big project to succeed in a distributed fashion."

But Ted's not quite right, as Jim Gettys kindly pointed out to
me. In spring 1992, Orest Zborowsky had added the X Window
System to Linux. But what was that? Again, we've got to wander
back in time.

After receiving his Ph.D. from the University of Waterloo
and spending a few years teaching at the University of British
Columbia, David Cheriton moved to Stanford. There (in the
early-1980s) he began working on operating systems: Thoth and
Verax (which hardly anyone recalls) and V. V was a microkernel
OS with microthreading and synchronous message passing. But
parts of V were important.

The W Window System got its name because it was hosted
(on top of the VGTS Graphics Package) on V operating system,
and the X Window System got its name because its first version
was based on W. Note: V -> W -> X. That simple.

By 1987, X Windows was important. And the system had
become increasingly widespread. Gettys' chronology (USENIX
meeting, June 2000) runs:

1984–86:	X1-X10
1987–88:	X11
1988–92:	GUI Wars (founding of the X Consortium)
1993–96:	"the Dark Ages"
1996–2000:	Linux and *BSD development; new toolkits; applications
2000– :	modern times

Gettys, at MIT in the late 1980s, was one of the first X Windows developers. And he remained at Athena and the X Consortium until he went to Compaq in the late 1990s. He is now vice-president at OLPC.[1]

In much of this development, Keith Packard played an important role. Moving to MIT from Oregon in 1988, he spent 1988–92 at the X Consortium, then returning to Oregon to work on X terminals at NCD. From 1999, he worked on XFree86 for SUSE and then (2001–2005) in Cambridge at the Compaq (and HP) labs, until they were shut down. He now works for Intel.

Packard is responsible for a vast number of extensions (including XRender, XFixes, XRandR), KDrive, fontconfig, and Nickle.

Nickle, Packard writes, "is a programming language based prototyping environment with powerful programming and scripting capabilities. Nickle supports a variety of datatypes, especially arbitrary precision numbers. The programming language vaguely resembles C."

All of us — even those running a Microsoft system — are running X Windows. Our debts to Gettys, Packard and many other contributors[2] are untold.

---

[1] See the footnote about OLPC on page 161.
[2] The XFree86 X manual page says "A cast of thousands, literally."

22 Tanenbaum and Torvalds

Linus posted his queries, his information and his work on comp.os.minix beginning in mid-1991. But on 29 January 1992, Andy Tanenbaum posted a note with the line: Subject: LINUX is obsolete.[1]

After a few introductory paragraphs, Tanenbaum got to his real criticism of Linux:

> As a result of my occupation, I think I know a bit about where operating systems are going in the next decade or so. Two aspects stand out:
>
> Microkernel vs Monolithic System
>
> Most older operating systems are monolithic, that is, the whole operating system is a single a.out file that runs in 'kernel mode.' This binary contains the process management, memory management, file system and the rest. Examples of such systems are UNIX, MS-DOS, VMS, MVS, OS/360, MULTICS, and many more.

---

[1] A large collection of the correspondence — or at least that of the "major" contributors — can be found at ftp://ftp.funet.fi/pub/Linux/doc/news/ Linux_is_obsolete.Z As I am interested in discussing this, I will refrain from extensive citation. A "dead tree" version of much of the discussion is available as Appendix A of *Open Sources: Voices from the Open Source Revolution* (O'Reilly, 1999; ISBN 1565925823).

The alternative is a microkernel-based system, in which most of the OS runs as separate processes, mostly outside the kernel. They communicate by message passing. The kernel's job is to handle the message passing, interrupt handling, low-level process management, and possibly the I/O. Examples of this design are the RC4000, Amoeba, Chorus, Mach, and the not-yet-released Windows/NT.

While I could go into a long story here about the relative merits of the two designs, suffice it to say that among the people who actually design operating systems, the debate is essentially over. Microkernels have won. The only real argument for monolithic systems was performance, and there is now enough evidence showing that microkernel systems can be just as fast as monolithic systems (e.g., Rick Rashid has published papers comparing Mach 3.0 to monolithic systems) that it is now all over but the shoutin`.

MINIX is a microkernel-based system. The file system and memory management are separate processes, running outside the kernel. The I/O drivers are also separate processes (in the kernel, but only because the brain-dead nature of the Intel CPUs makes that difficult to do otherwise). LINUX is a monolithic style system. This is a giant step back into the 1970s. That is like taking an existing, working C program and rewriting it in BASIC. To me, writing a monolithic system in 1991 is a truly poor idea.

Linus responded the same day with: "Time for some serious flamefesting!" and a long (somewhat intemperate, but this is a 23-year old student) response.

There was a good deal of going back and forth, and even Brian Kernighan put in a few lines. But the result was that Andy remains to this day a committed microkernel devotee and Linus has continued with a largely monolithic system. (Of course, this generalization is inaccurate, but it serves.)

And, on a certain level, there is no question in my mind but that Andy's position is right: microkernels are "better" than monolithic systems. But, on the other hand, I find both Andy's original posting unnecessarily rebarbative and Linus' "serious flamefesting" inappropriate.

Over a decade later, I find it hard to discern any anger or resentment on either side. I asked Andy about the exchange, but he just shrugged me off. "In a straight test," he later remarked, "Linux loses by about 8% in speed." That may well be true. But it's not much of an epitaph.

However, I still think the microkernel is superior to the monolithic kernel — I guess I'll now be subject to a flame war.

The Daemon, the Gnu, and the Penguin

23 Proliferating Penguins

From the early 1980s on, the big gripe about UNIX was that it had split and resplit, that there were just too many variants. The fact that they had a common base was irrelevant to the critics – and many (if not most) of those critics were selling VMS or MVS or DOS or ...

Following Linus' postings of 1991, there soon were what we have come to call "distributions." And, rather than utilizing ftp, they came on CD-ROM.

The first of these was Adam Richter's Yggdrasil (in the Old Norse *Edda*, Yggdrasil is the "world ash," from a branch of which Odin/Wotan made his spear). Yggdrasil alpha was released on 8 December 1992. It was called LGX: Linux/GNU/X — the three components of the system. Recall that Gilmore, Tiemann and Henkel-Wallace formed Cygnus in 1989. Richter spoke to Michael Tiemann about setting up a business, but was "definitely uninterested in joining forces with Cygnus."

Yggdrasil beta was released the next year. Richter's press release read:

> The Yggdrasil beta release is the first UNIX(R) clone
> to include multimedia facilities as part of its base con-
> figuration. The beta release also includes X-windows,
> networking ... an easy installation mechanism, and
> the ability to run directly from the CD-ROM.

The beta was priced at $50; the production release was $99.

SuSE was formed in 1992 also, as a consulting group (SuSE was originally S.u.S.E., which stood for "Software- und System-Entwicklung," Software and System Development), but did not release a Linux distribution for several years. The next distribution — and the oldest still in existence — was Patrick Volkerding's Slackware, released 16 July 1993, soon after he graduated from Minnesota State University Moorhead.

Slackware, in turn, was the basis for SuSE's release "Linux 1.0" of SLS/Slackware in 1994. (SLS was "Softlanding Linux System," Peter McDonald's 1992 distribution, on which parts of Slackware were based.) SuSE later integrated Florian La Roche's Jurix, yielding a unique distribution: SuSE 4.2 (1996).

The next year, Mark Bolzern was trying to sell a UNIX database from Multisoft, a German company. He encountered difficulties because it was relatively expensive to set up the UNIX system. Then he came across Gnu/Linux and realized that he now had a real solution. He convinced Multisoft to port Flagship (the db) to Linux and "that was the first commercial product released on Linux," Bolzern said. "People were always having trouble installing Linux," he continued, "and then Flagship wouldn't run right because something had changed." Bolzern decided that what was needed was a release that wouldn't change for a year, so he "picked a specific distribution of Slackware" and "the name Linux Pro." Soon he was selling more Linux than Flagship: "we're talking hundreds per month."

And when Red Hat came out, Bolzern picked that up.

Marc Ewing had set up Red Hat in 1993. He said: "I started Red Hat to produce a development tool I thought the world needed. Linux was just becoming available and I used [it] as my development platform. However, I soon found that I was spending more time managing my Linux box than I was developing my software, and I concluded that what the world really needed was a good Linux distribution ... "[1]

In 1993, Bob Young was working for Vernon Computer Rentals. He told me: "I knew the writing was on the wall for my future with that company." He continued:

---

[1]See Glyn Moody, *Rebel Code* (Perseus Publishing, 2001), p. 97.

Red Hat the company was legally incorporated in March of 1993 in Connecticut under the name: ACC Corp. Inc. It changed its name to Red Hat Software, Inc. in early 1996, and changed its name a last time to simply Red Hat, Inc. just before going public in June of 1999.

ACC Corp. Inc. bought the assets, including all copyrights and trademarks (none were registered at the time) relating to Marc Ewing's sole proprietorship business venture in January 1993. Marc's Red Hat project was not incorporated but was run out of Marc's personal checking account. Marc received shares in ACC Corp, Inc. in return for the Red Hat name and assets.

In 1995 Red Hat packaged Linux, some utilities and initial support for $50. Also in 1995, Bryan Sparks (with funding from Ray Noorda, former CEO of Novell) founded Caldera and The Apache Foundation released Apache, which would become the most widespread Web server. But Red Hat soon became the most popular Linux release. This was unexpected: Linus had said that he expected Caldera to be the top supplier, because it was "kind of a step beyond," in that it was targeting the office market. "I think what's interesting about Caldera is they based their stuff on Red Hat and then they added a commercial kind of approach."

When Red Hat became a "success," Bob Young and family moved from Connecticut to North Carolina (Ewing lived in Durham).

It was the end of July 1996. Just in time for Hurricane Fran, the first hurricane to visit Raleigh since hurricane Hazel in 1954. Yes, "the" hurricane Hazel that is the only hurricane to make it to southern Ontario still categorized as a hurricane that I know of.

(Before abandoning this, I should point out that Young is from Hamilton, Ont., and attended the University of Toronto. During the night of October 18, 1954, "Hurricane Hazel pelted Toronto with rain and killed 81 people. On one street alone, Raymore Drive, 35 neighbors were drowned." [Environment Canada, Canadian Hurricane Centre, Storms of 1954.])

ACC, Young's company, sold Linux/UNIX software and books. Young had been introduced to the UNIX world in 1988, when he was with Vernon Leasing and Rentals, and began publishing *New York UNIX* as well as catalog sales. This led to his being the founding editor of *Linux Journal*, a post he held for two issues in 1994, before "splitting the losses" with Phil Hughes.

In May 1994, Linus was invited by Kurt Reisler, the UniSIG Chairman, to speak at a DECUS conference in New Orleans. This was funded by Digital's marketing group at the suggestion of Jon "maddog" Hall. It was at this conference that maddog first saw Linux running on a PC, and he immediately thought of porting it to an Alpha system, which was then the fastest 64-bit micro-processor on the market.

Linux was, for the most part, a 32-bit system, and while it had been ported to other processors, the code tree that Linus worked on concentrated on Intel-based processors. Having the same code tree span both 32 and 64 bit processors as well as various architectures would ensure that the kernel would stay "portable."

maddog returned to his office in New Hampshire, arranged for an Alpha workstation to be shipped to Linus in Helsinki, and then helped pull together an engineering group to assist with the port.

Linus returned to the United States in June 1994 to attend a USENIX conference in Boston, and while he munched on a hotdog, he signed the "Loan of Products" paper that would allow him to use the Alpha. When he asked if he would have to return it, maddog responded that he had never seen a "Loan of Products" returned.

Linus received the Alpha, along with many electronic manuals about the Alpha architecture, but did not really start the port until he had finished the next release of the kernel. In the meantime Linus was thinking about how to structure the code, and the code tree.

In January 1995 the actual port was begun, and by November, Red Hat had put out a binary release of their distribution that ran on the Alpha processors.

The bulk of this work came from the community, with people buying fairly expensive Alpha processors and systems just so they could help with the port.

In the summer of 1995, I was approached by Lisa Bloch, then the Executive Director of the FSF, as to the feasibility of a conference on "Freely Redistributable Software." I was enthusiastic, but had my qualms about profitability. Richard, at our meeting, was quite understanding: FSF would bankroll the affair, but he hoped we could turn a small profit.

Lisa and I put together a committee (Bob Chassell, Chris Demetriou, John Gilmore, Kirk McKusick, Rich Morin, Eric Raymond, and Vernor Vinge) and we posted a Call for Papers on several newsgroups.

Thanks to maddog, Linus agreed to be one keynote speaker, Stallman was the other. We had a day of tutorials and two days of papers. February 3–5, 1996, at the Cambridge Center Marriott. Amazingly, everything ran smoothly. By the end, I was a nervous wreck. And the FSF ended up making a tiny profit.

The Daemon, the Gnu, and the Penguin

24 Yet more Penguins

Debian Linux, as I stated in Chapter 21, was created by Ian Murdock. He officially founded the "Project" on August 16, 1993. From November 1994 to November 1995 the Debian Project was sponsored by the FSF.

In November 1995, Infomagic released an experimental version of Debian which was only partially in ELF format as "Debian 1.0."[1] On December 11, Debian and Infomagic jointly announced that this release "was screwed." Bruce Perens, who had succeeded Murdock as "leader," said that the data placed on the 5-CD set would most likely not even boot properly.

The real result was that the "real" release, "Buzz ," was 1.1 (June 17, 1996), with 474 packages. Bruce was employed by Pixar and so all Debian releases are named after characters in *Toy Story* (1995). So the next decade saw:

- 1.2 Rex, December 12, 1996 (848 packages)

- 1.3 Bo, June 5, 1997 (974 packages)

- 2.0 Hamm, July 24, 1998 ("over 1500 packages")

- 2.1 Slink, March 9, 1999 ("about 2250 packages")

- 2.2 Potato, August 15, 2000 ("more than 3900 binary packages")

- 3.0 Woody, July 19, 2002 (8500 binary packages)

---

[1] ELF is the Executable and Linkable Format. It is (now) the standard file format for all Unix-derivative systems except Mac OS X. It is part of the Tool Interface Standard.

- 3.1 Sarge, June 6, 2005 (15,400 packages)

- 4.0 Etch, April 8, 2007 (18,000 packages)

Buzz fit on one CD. Slink went to two. Sarge required 14 CDs in the official set. It was released fully translated to over 30 languages and contains a new Debian-Installer. Slink had also introduced ports to the Alpha and Sparc. In 1999, Debian also began a Hurd port.

Though Debian carried the burden of being tough to install for several years, Sarge has changed that. The new installer with automatic hardware detection is quite remarkable.

I introduced Red Hat in Chapter 20, and I will return to the company again, but at this point I'd like to introduce Mandrake, a Linux distribution based on Red Hat 5.1 and KDE (originally, the Kool Desktop Environment, now the K Desktop Environment). It was created by Gael Duval, a graduate of Caen University, in July 1998. From 1998 to early 2004, Mandrake was reasonably successful, for several reasons: it was notable for its high degree of internationalization as well as for the variety of chips it would run on. However, in February 2004 MandrakeSoft lost a suit filed by the Hearst Syndicate which claimed invasion of their trademarked "Mandrake the Magician."[2] Starting with 10.0, there was a minor name change. Then, in April 2005, MandrakeSoft announced that there was a merger with Conectiva, and that the new name would be Mandriva.

Joseph Cheek founded Redmond Linux in 2000. In 2001 it merged with DeepLinux. In January 2002 the company was renamed Lycoris and its Desktop/LX was based on Caldera's Workstation 3.1. In June 2005, Lycoris was acquired by Mandriva.

I've gone through all this to show just how complex the tale of Linux distributions can be. And, as of this writing, there appear

---

[2]Mandrake the Magician, first published in 1934, was the original "caped crusader," preceding Superman by four years.

to be well over 350 distributions. I will neither enumerate nor elaborate on most of them. However, the most "popular" appear to be:

- Red Hat

- Fedora

- Debian

- Gentoo

- Knoppix

- SuSE/SUSE (now Novell)

- Slackware

- TSL

- Yellow Dog

- Mandriva

- College Linux

- Ubuntu

It might be a full-time job to track all the distributions and fully describe their origins.

For instance, Kanotix is a Debian derivative. It is also a Knoppix derivative, as it is a live CD.[3] And it is solid as a rock.

Knoppix was created by Klaus Knopper, a freelance IT/Linux consultant. It has achieved popularity because it is easily run from the CD, without installation, and because it can be readily employed to fix corrupted file systems, etc. It was the first Linux available on a live CD.

---

[3]A live CD is a bootable, read-only compact disk that contains an operating system that can be loaded into memory so that the computer can be operated without the necessity of mounting anything on the hard drive.

In 1996 Bob Young and Red Hat moved corporate headquarters to North Carolina. In January 1997, Greylock and August Capital invested $6.25 million in Cygnus Solutions, becoming the first VCs to invest in a free software business. In July, Red Hat 4.2 was released and, in December, 5.0 was announced.

These are important events as could be seen in November 1998, when a Microsoft lawyer waved a Red Hat box in the air in federal court to "refute" the US Justice Department charge that Microsoft had a monopoly on the desktop operating system market.

While Red Hat may not have been the most innovative company, they had already become the iconic Linux enterprise in the public's eye.

In August of 1999 Red Hat had its IPO, the eighth largest first day gain in Wall Street history. (On 9 December 1999, VA Linux had its IPO.) And in November 1999, Red Hat acquired Cygnus, creating the largest "open source" company in the world.

Just how successful Linux and some Linux companies had become was made obvious at the outset of the new millennium:

- In January 2001 Scott McNealy said that Linux is a "better NT than NT";

  and

- In February 2001 Steve Ballmer called Linux "a cancer" and "an intellectual property destroyer."

Oh, boy!

25 Oceans of FUD

When Gene Amdahl coined the acronym "FUD"[1] in the mid-1970s, his ire was aimed at Frank Cary, chairman of the Board at IBM, who was waging a no-holds-barred attack on Amdahl, Itel, Control Data, and the other small companies that were selling machines that competed with the IBM 360/168.

According to history professor Robert Sobel,[2]

> The campaign began in a conventional fashion. IBM salesmen and executives visited clients who were thought to be considering plug-compatible machines, to warn them of problems that might arise should Amdahl or National Semicomputer leave the business. There was talk of reduced maintenance on IBM peripheral equipment hooked onto other mainframes, of software changes to eliminate or reduce compatibility, and of alterations in hardware that could make the Amdahls less compatible than advertised.

Sound familiar?

By the end of 1997, Eric Raymond had delivered "The Cathedral and the Bazaar" at least twice: at Linux Kongress in May and at the Perl Conference in November. It appeared in *First Monday* online in 1998, on paper in *Matrix News* in three installments (June, July and August 1998), and in book form in 1999. It does not seem to have been read in Redmond, Wash.

---

[1]Fear, Uncertainty and Doubt

[2]*IBM: Colossus in Transition* (Times Books, 1981), chapter 15.

The Daemon, the Gnu, and the Penguin

In the May 1999 issue of *Microsoft Internet Developer*, Douglas Boling wrote:

> While free distribution is a great marketing tool (think about all those samples you get in the mail), what does it say about the product itself? Frankly, it says that the product (or the effort that went into making the product) has no value. Is that what you software engineers out there want? ...If ...you gave away all software, how would you pay the creators of that software?

Boling goes on, but I'll spare my readers. I was also going to cite Microsoft's "Linux myths," but those pages are no longer accessible at http://www.microsoft.com/ntserver/nts/news/msnw/LinuxMyths/asp.

It was there I read that there were "hundreds of UNIX vendors with no 'standard' flavor of UNIX" (take that, POSIX!). And that "Windows NT 4.0 Outperforms Linux on Common Customer Workloads" (which stemmed from an inability of the Linux stack to handle multiple network cards on SMP machines adequately — the vital "Customer Workload").

But in August 1999 Red Hat had its IPO and, by Christmas, it had acquired Cygnus, and VA Linux Systems had had its IPO. Free software was becoming big business.

But then, so was nearly everything else. Pets.com, boo.com, and a variety of other fantasies blew hundreds of millions of dollars.

In 1999 we were nearly at the peak of what was (retrospectively) known as the Dot-Com bubble: the dot-bomb. But a look at history is needed.

NASDAQ was begun in 1951. By 1990 it was a good-sized marketplace with a large number of new and recently-formed corporations holding their IPOs. Many of these were hi-tech; many were in areas previously untested: selling products over the Internet, setting up and using Web sites, indulging in e-commerce, rather than selling products in shops. Some of the new companies were actually involved in Information Technology, rather than using it. But they all showed great promise, and folks didn't want to miss the boat.

After the stock market crash of 1987 (in which the Dow-Jones average dropped 22.6% and lost about $500 billion on October 19), the markets around the world continued their bullish ways. In the early 1990s, the personal computer was becoming a household object and the advent of the Web made access yet more user-friendly. 1994 saw the business world "discover" the Internet as a commercial opportunity, and yet more companies were formed. Amazon began in 1994; eBay in 1995. On December 5, 1996, Alan Greenspan warned of "irrational exhuberance" as evidenced by the rapidly-rising stock prices.

In 1997, NASDAQ announced a new listing standard: it would base new listings on market capitalization alone, basically telling the world that accounting regulations had hindered many new firms, preventing them from listing. There was a surge of registrations. In fact, "nearly 50% of the new listings between Aug 1997 and June 2000 entered under the market capitalization standard." [3] In other words, profit/loss statements, assets, and corporate governance no longer meant anything. Only "market capitalization" (price times number of shares) meant anything. Tulip bulbs were back.

Greenspan's warning didn't count. From 1996 to 2000, NASDAQ soared from 600 to 5000. And then it crashed. On March 10, 2000, the NASDAQ fell from its peak of 5132.52. Within six weeks, NASDAQ dropped from 5000 to 2000, then to 800 (in 2002). MicroStrategy, a soaring business-software provider, fell

---

[3] I am indebted to the extensive analysis of April Klein and Partha Mohanram, "They Came, they Conquered, they Collapsed" (March 2005) for much of the following.
See http://papers.ssrn.com/sol3/papers.cfm?abstract_id=680667

from $3500 per share to $4, the victim of an accounting scam. On December 14, 2000, it was at $15.19.

The emperor had no clothes.

Over five years later, at the end of 2005, NASDAQ had climbed back to 2200. In October 2006, it had still not achieved 50% of its 2000 peak. Even Microsoft dropped from over $60/share to $20/share in 2000–2001, shedding two-thirds of its (paper) value. It closed 2005 at under 50% of its peak.[4]

Looking at Klein and Mohanram again, "367 non-financial firms [were] listed under the Type 3 criteria between ... August 1997 and the end of the hi-tech IPO boom in June 2000. Without this alternative, none of these 367 firms would have entered the NNM [NASDAQ National Market] on their entry date." Moreover, "over a four-year event-time window, Type 3 firms earn significantly less than other NNM new listings ... "

Klein and Mohanram illustrate that the inflation of the bubble (and its bursting) were not merely "irrational exhuberance," but specifically an "irrational exhuberance" concerning barely-understood yet extensively hyped hi-tech ventures. No idea was too bizarre to invest in. (More tulips, anyone?)

These last few paragraphs are a background. The rise and ebb of FUD has consistently followed the rise and fall of the stock market or the rise and fall of (perceived) commercial threats. Thirty years ago, the rise of "other" mainframes worried IBM. The collapse of its stock price worried Microsoft. So did the fact that new offerings were not really in the offing.

One of the useful forms of past FUD had been "preannouncement": press concerning wonders of the future. Following the drop in the NASDAQ market, here's what appeared in *The Register* where Microsoft is concerned:

- July 27, 2001: "an intermediate release ... dubbed 'Longhorn' will ... slip out late next year or early 2003."

---

[4]And at the beginning of 2008, NASDAQ was at 2300 and Microsoft at $30/share.

- August 7, 2001: "the next release of Windows Server, code-named Longhorn and due in mid 2003 ... "

- October 24, 2001: "the wheels have come off the Windows rollout wagon ... "

- May 8, 2003: "It will assuredly be stuff that's in Longhorn ...but we detect bits that must currently be missing, and that will be hard, if not impossible, to execute by 2004."

- August 27, 2004: "Microsoft project managers have demanded that features be jettisoned in order for the next major version of Windows to ship as projected by 2006 ... "

- May 19, 2005: "Gartner says the first Longhorn client could slip into 2007 ... "

But then, on July 22, 2005, Microsoft issued a press release: "**Media Alert:** Microsoft Unveils Official Name for 'Longhorn' and Sets Date for First Beta Targeted at Developers and Professionals." The name was Vista. The new date of release was August 3, 2005.

I wrote that in November 2006, still waiting for Vista (aka Longhorn). But, lo!, on November 8, 2006, the Associated Press reported: "Microsoft Corp. said Wednesday it has completed work on its long-delayed Windows Vista operating system and plans to release it to consumers January 30.

"The announcement means Microsoft is on track to meet its revised release schedule." (By my tally, it's Microsoft's revised, revised, revised, revised, revised "release schedule." But I may have missed one or two.)

What's the function of this?

Let's suppose that you're the CIO or CTO reporting to the CEO of a Fortune 1000 company. Microsoft targets its marketing pitch at that CEO. Your company is going to invest lots of cash: dollars, yen, pounds, euros. Do you take a chance on the unknown (Mandriva, SUSE, Red Hat) or stay with the familiar (known to your CEO) and wait? Remember: No one ever got fired for buying IBM, XEROX, etc. That's what they used to say. (*Note*: Vista was, indeed, released on January 30, 2007.)

Preannouncement is one tactic; planting "news" is another; questioning *bonae fides* is a third.

As an illustration, here are some data from 2003:

- March 2003. Caldera (dba The SCO Group) files suit against IBM in 3rd Judicial District, Salt Lake County, court.

- March 25, 2003. The case is "removed" to Federal jurisdiction.

- May 29, 2003. Chris Sontag, SCO Group's "senior vice president and general manager of SCOsource Division," tells Patrick Thibodeau of *Computerworld:* "There is no mechanism in Linux to ensure [the legality of the] intellectual property being contributed by various people .... I would suspend any new Linux activities until this is all sorted out."

- The 1Q2003 Caldera filing with the SEC reveals nearly $10 million income from two license sales: to Microsoft and Sun.

- October 16, 2003: Press Release: "$50 Million Private Investment Transaction Led by BayStar Capital Provides SCO With Funding for ... and the Protection of the Company's Intellectual Property Assets." (This was later altered to "from Two Investors including BayStar Capital ..." The SEC 8K and purchase agreement reveals the second [larger] PIPE investor to be the Royal Bank of Canada.)

License fees, private equity investments. Shoring up confidence in a company; raising questions for potential customers; stalling for time when an OS is delayed; paying the lawyers (Boies, Schiller & Flexner received a $31million fee from The SCO Group).

Nearly a year earlier, in 2002, the Alexis de Tocqueville Institution issued a white paper using the terms "'terrorism' and 'national security' [in a] shameful attempt to use fear, uncertainty and doubt to push Microsoft's monopolistic agenda"; the paper, "Opening the Open Source Debate," is no longer accessible.[5] Only one correspondent, Kenneth Brown, challenged Forno's view. But in May 2004, the Institution and Mr. Brown resurfaced. This time, Brown put out a "study" which revealed that Linus Torvalds wasn't the father of Linux at all. Here's a part of the press release[6]

> In one of the few extensive and critical studies on the source of open source code, Kenneth Brown, president of AdTI, traces the free software movement over three decades — from its romantic but questionable beginnings, through its evolution to a commercial effort that draws on unpaid contributions from thousands of programmers.

> Among other points, the study directly challenges Linus Torvalds' claim to be the inventor of Linux.

> Brown's account is based on extensive interviews with more than two dozen leading technologists in the United States, Europe, and Australia, including Richard Stallman, Dennis Ritchie, and Andrew Tanenbaum.

> "The report," according to Gregory Fossedal, a Tocqueville senior fellow, "raises important questions that all developers and users of open source code must face.

> "One cannot group all open source programmers together. Many are rigorous and respectful of intellectual property. Others, though, speak of intellectual

---

[5]Richard Forno in *Security Focus*, June 19, 2002
[6]http://www.adti.net/kenarbeit/samiz.release.html

property rights — at least when it comes to the property of others — with open contempt."

Fossedal, incidentally, was the author of "Opening the Open Source Debate."

Linus responded, saying it was true, he had been found out, "The true fathers of Linux are Santa Claus and the Tooth Fairy" [*LinuxWorld* May 17, 2004].

Andy Tanenbaum was less easy-going: "Brown is not the sharpest knife in the drawer," he posted.

While listed as a 124-page E-Book, Mr. Brown's opus is "not yet available," over 48 months after the press release. (Oh, yes. By the way: Microsoft has been a supporter of the Alexis de Tocqueville Institution "for at least five years." Now, watch me pull a rabbit out of this hat . . .)

Rounding this off, it is worth re-reading what Dennis Ritchie wrote a decade ago. After several years' effort, Dennis and I had succeeded in amassing permissions where Lions' *Code and Commentary* was concerned. In his brief foreword for the volume, he said:

> : . . . The fundamental tension — how to publish software, comment on it, encourage learning from it, yet still retain commercial and technical control — still has not been resolved, and doubtless has no resolution. The Free Software Foundation wants all software available in source. Most of academia agrees in principle, but even there, important factions want to retain rights and make some money. The commercial world wants to guard rights carefully and make a lot of money. Over the years, UNIX has somehow steered a turbulent, sometimes crazily anarchic middle course.[7]

---

[7] *Lions' Commentary on UNIX 6th Edition with Source Code* (Peer-to-Peer Communications, 1996), p. x.

In general, FUD has quite limited utility. In the 1970s it could be somewhat effective. The growth of the Internet has reduced that: reality moves around at the speed of light. And while Don Basilio (in Gioachino Rossini's "The Barber of Seville") was right about rumors, technology has caught up with the ability to promulgate FUD.

In November 2007, an Australian interviewer asked Linus:

> Do you think there is any way Microsoft, patent holders, or lawyers can take direct aim at the kernel development process and impede it?

He responded:

> I really don't know. I don't think they can impede the technology, and I really don't think there is anything real behind that whole intellectual property FUD machine. But nearly infinite amounts of money certainly goes a long way.[8]

---

[8]Charles Babcock in *iTnews*,
   http://www.itnews.com.au/Feature/4052,
   torvalds-on-where-linux-is-headed-in-2008.aspx

The Daemon, the Gnu, and the Penguin

Excursus: What's in a Name?

Linux is a kernel.

The first distributions (1992) were labeled "Linux/GNU/X" – recognizing the kernel, the tools, and the windowing system. When the Debian Project was established in 1994, it called the "system" "Debian GNU/Linux."

The *GNU Bulletin* of June 1994, called Linux "a free UNIX clone," but the next issue of the *Bulletin* in January 1995, employed "GNU/Linux."

In 1996, the FSF released Emacs 19.31. It was tuned for (Stallman's coinage) "Lignux." The term was not picked up widely, and was dropped with a year. Stallman and the FSF have continued to employ "GNU/Linux."

In 1996 Linus posted:

> From: torva...@linux.cs.Helsinki.FI (Linus Torvalds)
> Subject: Lignux, what's the matter with you people?
> Date: 1996/06/03
> Message-ID: 4ounl9$1mf@linux.cs.Helsinki.FI#1/1X-
> Deja-AN: 158302270
> content-type: text/plain; charset=ISO-8859-1
> organization: A Red Hat Commercial Linux Sitemime-
> version: 1.0
> newsgroups: gnu.misc.discuss,comp.os.linux.misc
>
> Umm,
>
> this discussion has gone on quite long enough, thank you very much. It doesn't really _matter_ what peo-

ple call Linux, as long as credit is given where credit is due (on both sides). Personally, I'll very much continue to call it "Linux", but there have already been distributions that call it "Linux Pro(tm)" etc, which I don't find all that surprising ...

The GNU people tried calling it GNU/Linux, and that's ok. It's certainly no worse a name than "Linux Pro" or "Red Hat Linux" or "Slackware Linux" (the last two are often just called "Red Hat" and "Slackware" when talking among Linux people, so there the "Linux" part has fallen off altogether).

Lignux is just a punny name — I think Linux/GNU or GNU/Linux is a bit more "professional" myself, but I'm not going to get gray hairs about this.

Much worse than the strange name is all the silly newsgroup and email activity this has resulted in. It's not as if the FSF unilaterally changed the name of the OS — they just changed the name of their "distribution" (well, it seems it's currently just GNU emacs for Linux, but maybe this will be a trend).

Btw, I've often been irritated by the "unknown" in the gcc setups for Linux, and I'd much rather see a gcc calling itself "i586-gnu-linux" than "i586-unknown-linux" any day (but I have to admit that either is preferable to "lignux" in this context ;-).

Relax,

Linus

The next year, Stallman wrote:

Through a peculiar turn of events, the version of GNU which is widely used today is more often known as "Linux", and many users are not aware of the extent of its connection with the GNU Project.

There really is a Linux, and these people are using it, but it is not the operating system. Linux is the kernel: the program in the system that allocates the machine's resources to the other programs that you run. The kernel is an essential part of an operating system, but useless by itself; it can only function in the context of a complete operating system. Linux is normally used in a combination with the GNU operating system: the whole system is basically GNU, with Linux functioning as its kernel. [www.gnu.org/gnu/linux-and-gnu.html]

It might be worth looking at two definitions at this point, the 3rd edition of *The New Hacker's Dictionary* (MIT Press, 1996), p. 340, s.v. **operating system**, says:

The foundation software of a machine, of course; that which schedules tasks, allocates storage, and presents a default interface to the user between applications.

The ISO *Vocabulary for Data Processing* (Technical Committee 97), defines **operating system** as:

Software that controls the execution of programs; an operating system may provide services such as resource allocation, scheduling, input/output control, and data management.

Under these definitions, there is no "GNU operating system." The services in the definitions are provided by Linux. The Hurd has never been much more than the FSF's name for the servers running the Mach microkernel to implement file systems, network protocols, file access control, and other features that are implemented by the Unix kernel or similar kernels (such as Linux). (www.gnu.org/software/hurd/hurd.html)

Of course, one could cite Stan Kelly-Bootle's definition in the 2nd edition of *The Computer Contradictionary* (MIT Press, 1995), p. 154: "That part of the system that inhibits operation."

In the "jargon file," Eric Raymond wrote (2003):

> (Some people object that the name 'Linux' should be used to refer only to the kernel, not the entire operating system. This claim is a proxy for an underlying territorial dispute; people who insist on the term GNU/Linux want the FSF to get most of the credit for Linux because RMS and friends wrote many of its user-level tools. Neither this theory nor the term GNU/Linux has gained more than minority acceptance).

The FSF has made many contributions to what we think of as the Red Hat or SUSE or Knoppix or Ubuntu distributions. If you run Solaris, you run code originated at Bell Labs, at UC Berkeley, at many other sites, and ... even ... at Sun Microsystems. Calling it BTL/UCB/Solaris has never come up. This neither lessens FSF's nor UCB's contributions. (In fact, nearly everything you receive when you purchase a Microsoft "system" was created by another entity — and either purchased or pilfered by Microsoft.)

After all, if I purchase a car or a computer just how many components are manufactured by the company identified on the nameplate? In fact, if I said I'd bought an Intel or an AMD or a PowerPC box all I've done is identify a chip. And if I say I'm running Linux (or GNU/Linux) on an Intel box, it doesn't reveal a great deal.

These worries all stem from bourgeois formalism.

There's also the question of free vs. open software. I admit that I stand with Stallman on the free side, not with Raymond and O'Reilly on the open side. GPLv3 (2007) provides me with the most current "argument":[1]

---

[1] This is from *A Quick Guide to GPLv3* available at http://www.gnu.org/licenses/quick-guide-gplv3.html.

Nobody should be restricted by the software they use. There are four freedoms that every user should have:

- the freedom to use the software for any purpose,
- the freedom to share the software with your friends and neighbors,
- the freedom to change the software to suit your needs, and
- the freedom to share the changes you make.

When a program offers users all of these freedoms, we call it free software.

Yep.

The Daemon, the Gnu, and the Penguin

26 Advanced Capitalism

In the "Introduction" to this book I mentioned Joseph Schumpeter. Schumpeter's theory is that "the success of capitalism will lead to a form of corporatism and a fostering of values hostile to capitalism, especially among intellectuals. The intellectual and social climate needed to allow entrepreneurship to thrive will not exist in advanced capitalism; it will be replaced by socialism in some form." This is what has been referred to as creative destruction.[1]

In the computer industry, Microsoft is the epitome of the "old" capitalism. It envelops and constrains and produces notably inferior products. (Think of the joke as to where the 800 pound gorilla sits.) But what will take its place as "advanced capitalism"?

In 2006, Chris Anderson (editor in chief of *Wired*) published *The Long Tail*.[2] Anderson's book is, I think, crucial to an understanding of just what our world is becoming. It is the enunciation of how we will advance.[3]

Anderson uses the worlds of books, movies and music to make his point. But I will limit myself to books here, as I think readers can easily extrapolate therefrom — and I believe that they will readily see the applicability of this to the world of computing.

The typical neighborhood bookstore carries 12,000 to 15,000

---

[1] *Capitalism, Socialism and Democracy* is still in print as a Harper Perennial, ISBN 0061330086.

[2] Hyperion Books. ISBN 1401302378.

[3] Nicholas Carr's *The Big Switch* (Norton, 2007; ISBN 0393062287) is another indicator.

titles. "The average Borders carries 100,000 titles. Yet about a quarter of Amazon's sales come from *outside* its top 100,000 titles." (Anderson, p. 23)

Let's put this in perspective. While current numbers are hard to obtain, *Publishers Weekly* reported the following for the US:

Year	Number of new titles
1990	46743
1991	48146
1992	49276
1993	42217
1994	51863
1995	62039
1996	58465
1997	64711

On 24 May 2005, Bowker (www.bowker.com) reported that "195,000 new titles and editions" had been published in the US in 2004. Apparently, about 50,000 titles are published each year in Canada. As a total list of available books includes older titles, the total number of books available in print is very large. Anderson notes that "If the Amazon statistics are any guide, the market for books that are not sold in the average bookstore is already a third the size of the existing market." Markets operate on "the economics of scarcity." Most companies aim their production and price their goods on the basis of what sells best. Yet, as Kevin Laws has said, "The biggest money is in the smallest sales."

Those smallest sales are what Anderson refers to as the "Long Tail markets."

Amazon takes advantage of this. So does Google, which does not earn most of its income from huge corporations (those advertise on the Super Bowl) but from small ones. EBay is a third long tail — vending collectors' items and rarities to individual buyers. Not vast quantities of knock-offs to the masses (like Wal-Mart and Target).

Note that all three of these have overcome the limitations of geography and of inventory size. Their sales are far outside the ambit of the physical retailer and they are far larger.

The ancestor of all this was Sears. Sears taught North America how to shop without a sales floor and without being able to touch what you were buying.

Sears, Roebuck and Co. was established in 1893. In 1894 it published a mail-order catalog of 322 pages. In 1895 it was 532 pages. The general public had learned how to buy sight unseen. And the catalogs could carry more varieties of merchandise and far more items than any general store could. In 1893 sales topped $400,000. In 1895 sales were over $750,000. In many ways, Sears anticipated selling a long tail.

The physical store has physical limitations; Amazon and its like do not.

What Richard Stallman initiated and what the free community have followed is quite definitely a form of socialism developed among intellectuals with a fostering of values hostile to capitalism. There is no question that entrepreneurism has flourished in this community: Cygnus, Red Hat, SuSE, etc. are all built on the long tail within a social climate built on sharing (not hoarding).

And look at the "other" side: the epitome of "old" capitalism is Microsoft. Growing by engulfing and emulating. Always late on the adoption of the new. The Internet was "irrelevant." Games and music were add-ons. Search engines were an afterthought. And most recently came the offer for Yahoo! — the last "old media" company. (And it goes for music and film as well – all the hullabaloo about copyright and piracy and DRM is a senile industry in its death-throes.)

Yahoo! owns or controls content, it markets to bring in audience and floods them with ads. Google arrives on my desktop with content, ads and tools. Yahoo! is centralized; Google is distributed. Microsoft, too, operates on an old control model — as I wrote above, it is the last of the "old" technology companies – controlled, closed . . . never open, never offering choice.

Think back. UNIX from AT&T originally ran only on DEC PDP machines. Then came the proliferation of hardware and the variety of UNIX systems. One of the big criticisms was the fact that there were so many "incompatible" UNIXes.

Then came Linux. And Linux runs on nearly every box, nearly every kind of chip. But (oh my!) there are so many different kinds – over 350 distributions. And there are a number of UNIXes as well. You're not compelled to run Vista. You can choose. You can opt.

Nicholas Carr, former editor of *The Harvard Business Review*, said "Microsoft makes its money selling licenses to millions and millions of people who install it on individual hard drives. Most of what you need is on the Internet — and it's free. There are early warning signs that the traditional Microsoft programs are losing their grip."[4]

A week earlier, John Markoff, a technology journalist, wrote: "In moving to buy Yahoo, Microsoft may be firing the final shot of yesterday's war .... Silicon Valley favors bottom-up innovation instead of growth by acquisition. The region's investment money and brain power are tuned to start-ups that can anticipate the next big thing rather than chase the last one."[5]

By the time you read this, the world will know more about these hot topics. But they serve as good examples.

---

[4]Cited in *The New York Times*, 9 February 2008.
[5]*The New York Times*, 3 February 2008.

27 Behavioral Economics

Dan Ariely is a professor at MIT who is interested in "behavioral economics" — the decisions we make everyday, when (say) shopping. But he doesn't assume that people make decisions rationally. He looks at different facets of life and examines people's expectations and their passions.

Ariely has written about his research[1], describing his many experiments. For example, to see how people treat money differently than non-money, he put 6-packs of Coke in college dorm refrigerators and figured out the "half-life of Coke" (i.e., how long it took for people to take [steal?] them). Quite quickly. He then left plates of money. No one took any.

Ariely's other experiments are similarly simple and clever. And he has produced a wonderful book. But that's not all. Much of what he describes is directly related to free and open source. Think about the experiment with the Coke. Clearly, for most people, when it comes to purchasing something, there is a big difference between free (as in "free beer") and even one cent.

Moreover, there is a big difference between how hard people will work for free (without pay) vs. different amounts of payment. People will work hard (such as moving furniture) for free (helping a friend move into a new place), and just as hard for lots of money (e.g., $60 per hour). They won't work as hard for a small amount (e.g., $2 per hour).

But Ariely distinguishes between the "social realm" and the "financial realm." When things move from the social realm to the financial realm they are viewed differently. People don't think:

---

[1]*Predictably Irrational* (New York: HarperCollins, 2008). ISBN 978-0-06-135323-9.

"This is the same as free, plus I'm getting a little bit of money."
They think "I'm being paid very little."

Dan Bricklin posted an interview with Ariely[2]. Here's Bricklin's "take":

> When comparing things, it is easier to compare things that are in the same "bucket". For example, it is easy to figure out what you would pay for a shirt similar to another you've bought previously. But if something is "free" or is in the social realm, then it is considered in a different bucket from the "money" realm and comparisons are done differently, as if you were comparing different types of items. They are different mindsets. When you switch from the money realm to another, things change and not just in ways related to price. So, Open Source software is often not compared head to head with proprietary software and other factors come into play when deciding its value.
>
> Feeling that your work is useful, even if you know it's an illusion, has motivational power with respect to that work.
>
> People have an over tendency to keep doors open: We love options and over value them. We love keeping our options open even when it is clearly not in our interest. The fact that a piece of software is Open Source, and thereby gives you options, is an attraction (such as being able to make changes yourself, even if you never actually take advantage of that option).
>
> ...Proprietary software has explicit contracts while Open Source software usually has incomplete social ones that are more flexible.

[2] http://danbricklin.com/log/2008_03_06.htm#ariely

Once you move from a social contract to a financial one, it's very hard to go back, so you have to be careful if you want to stay in the social realm ....

Open Source can be about the pride we take in our work and in the pride of knowing other people are taking what we've done and building upon it. Paying for the work, even paying some people but not others, can change that view and amount of pride for everybody ....

Just knowing a piece of software you are working on is covered by a socially helpful license (especially if it says it at the top of every file) may possibly affect your attitude while working on it. (This is my idea that stems from his research that says that just being asked to list some of the Ten Commandments cuts down cheating on subsequent tasks when compared to listing some book titles.)

We talked about the intoxicating "high" of doing programming.

He is interested in the meaning of labor. The old philosophy that you do a job just to be paid is wrong. However, we don't understand labor enough as an academic discipline — about passion, affiliation, and motivation. The area of Open Source software is interesting, he feels, because in many places it removes the issue of money and just leaves the "payment" of joy.

We overvalue what we have or what we create. Ownership or authorship moves things from financial-based to pride-based. The inefficiencies from the author's perspective of continuing to develop and support a project even after there are "better" alternatives could be very efficient for users worried about switching costs. These effects should be much

> stronger in Open Source than proprietary software
> because of the financial nature of deciding to keep
> proprietary software projects alive ....
>
> Open Source software removes money from the equa-
> tion and opens the opportunity to take other forces
> into account ....
>
> Finally, because of the way in which people do things
> by relative valuation and not absolute, he sees that
> the initial emerging social norms, such as in an Open
> Source community, are very strong and of long last-
> ing influence, since they become the baseline that
> future behavior is measured against.

This is, of course, exactly what Eric Raymond said nearly
a decade ago: we of the free/open software community are
not, in general, in it for the money. But we get a big ego boost
from contributing, from peer-recognition.[3] We earn what Cory
Doctorow refers to as "wuffie" — what we might think of as
reputation credits.[4]

And a decade before Raymond, Stallman was far more concerned with the use of software than with the profit from it.

---

[3]I wish that Ariely, Bricklin and Raymond would focus on free, rather than open
source. But I recognize that Tim O'Reilly and his band have overwhelmed
Stallman here.

[4]*Down and Out in the Magic Kingdom* (2003). ISBN 0765304368.

28 Sharing Access

In Chapter 16, I mentioned Cromix, CROMEMCO's UNIX clone. What I didn't mention there was that CROMEMCO had tried to license UNIX from AT&T, but had — thanks to the myopia of the lawyers – been summarily rejected.

Twenty years ago, Sun found its money-raising scheme of breaking out its C compiler thwarted because a cheaper (and better) compiler was available from the FSF. On the one hand, locking in your users offers some insurance where future sales are concerned. And that's the methodology Microsoft follows.

Using NT/XP/etc. entailed using Word, Excel, and a wide range of other applications. Purchasing an automobile didn't lock me in to a given brand of tires or sparkplugs; nor a specific radio or tape player; nor require me to purchase a specified brand of gasoline or diesel. Effectively, Microsoft did. (Various aspects of investigation, suit, court order, and review have been in process since 1990 [US Federal Trade Commission] and neither US court orders nor massive EU fines seem to have altered Microsoft's behavior.)

But then people found that they could, in fact, install other software (e.g. browsers other than IE). And when it was found that that software didn't work as well with Microsoft's operating system(s), they complained — loudly.

There are many possible instances, but the most recent I know of is OpenExchange by HP[1]: many companies rely on MS Exchange/Outlook integration; HP has now snatched away that previously-exclusive prop. This is truly important: MS needs

---

[1]No longer HP; was acquired by Zimbra, which was bought by Yahoo!. But irrelevant to the point here.

Windows (whatever its current "name" is) and Office for the company to survive. If they can't stranglehold the market into using Office, then they lose one of the primary reasons for people to use Windows at all. So to lose MS Office is to lose MS Windows is to lose the company. The Open Document Format (ODF) is a threat to that.[2]

Microsoft's problem isn't technical or financial or a matter of skill. It's attitudinal. Microsoft, from what I see, doesn't want to be interoperable with the GPL, their principal competition, or with ODF (which is an ISO standard) unless someone forces them. And that's not a problem we in the free/open community can fix for them. If they desired true interoperability, not customer lock in, they'd embrace ODF and work out one standard we could all employ, no matter what operating system we use. Think about the obvious goal of Microsoft's current patent strategy. It's the same song, to me. The GPL will be squeezed out, if Microsoft gets its way, and we all get squeezed for money whether we use Microsoft software or not.

This, of course, is why Microsoft remains in violation of the court decision on unbundling its operating system from its browser – NT or XP or Vista from Internet Explorer. To separate would mean that users would be able to choose. To opt for a different browser, Mozilla or Firefox, perhaps. Users might opt for OpenOffice or NeoOffice. Or something else.

There are many Microsoft shills among the computer press

---

[2]In April 2008, Microsoft's Office Open XML [the naming was not coincidental], having been submitted for 'fast track' approval by ISO by ECMA [a vendors' association], was voted a standard — despite the fact that a number of ballots have been protested and that Alex Brown, leader of the International Organization for Standardization (ISO) group in charge of maintaining the Office Open XML (OOXML) standard, revealed that Microsoft Office 2007 documents do not meet the latest specifications of the ISO OOXML draft standard. "Word documents generated by today's version of Microsoft Office 2007 do not conform to ISO/IEC 29500," said Brown. Four countries (Brazil, India, South Africa, and Venezuela) have filed formal protests of the process. This is an unprecedented situation in ISO. I have no idea what the result will be.

who refer to "benchmarks" to show how good Microsoft is. But look at the suite used. One benchmark runs:

- Adobe Photoshop CS2

- Autodesk 3ds max 8.0 SP-3

- Firefox 2

- Microsoft Office 2003 with SP-1

- Microsoft Windows Media Encoder 9.0

- Nero 7 Ultra Edition

- Roxio VideoWave Movie Creator 1.5

- WinZip Computing WinZip 10.0

Very well — I don't run any of these except Firefox. But how about an equivalent suite on a Linux PC using:

- The GIMP

- Blender

- Firefox 2

- OpenOffice 2.3

- AVIDemux

- K3b

- Kino and 'Q' DVD-Author

- File Roller

As near as I can tell, this second suite runs faster with no problems. By the time you read this, I may well be running a different set. I can pick and choose. And this ability brings "behavioral economics" into the picture. Cost may be a factor, but freedom is also a factor.

On 28 February 2008, *The New York Times* reported on the Sprint-Nextel merger:

> "Sprint reported losing $29.5 billion, or $10.36 per share, during the quarter ending Dec. 31. By comparison, Sprint Nextel earned $261 million, or 9 cents per share, during the same period a year ago.
>
> "The company said last month it would likely have to write off most of the remaining $30.7 billion in goodwill value from the acquisition of Nextel and a number of affiliates. Sprint Nextel has struggled since the purchase, plagued by technical problems, unfocused marketing and a difficulty in merging the two companies' work forces into a cohesive whole."

The ethos of the companies was a severe mismatch. Now look back at Chapter 25. What will happen if Microsoft attempts to swallow Yahoo!?[3] And what do those experiments of Dan Ariely in Chapter 27 tell us? They certainly don't expound great growth on the part of Microsoft. Nor do they bode a bright future for Yahoo!.

Let's look at a possible future.

---

[3] As of mid-July 2008 the battle between Yahoo! and Carl Icahn / Microsoft continued.

29 Where are We?

Recent figures estimate that Linux and other free/open software packages have increased their footprint to nearly 20% of all desktops. With the proliferation of One Laptop per Child (OLPC)[1], this will increase rapidly in the near future. But desktops are not the story. Google runs on Linux. So does Yahoo!. Many ISPs and banks run on BSD because of its impressive security.

As of 2007, Linux Online had tallied the following government/public sector users[2]

- German Bundesagentur fuer Arbeit (BA)
  (The German government's agency for labor)
- French Ministry for Education
- Library of Congress, USA
- Portuguese Ministry of Justice
- Swedish Armed Forces
- Government of Switzerland
- Berlin, Germany
- New Zealand's Inland Revenue

---

[1] One Laptop per Child is an organization founded by Nicholas Negroponte and a number of other connected with the MIT Media Lab. Announced in 2005 at the World Economic Forum, its basic notion involved a "$100" laptop. The basic notions of OLPC are stated to be: "OLPC espouses five core principles: (1) child ownership; (2) low ages; (3) saturation; (4) connection; and (5) free and open source." A number of "third world" countries and the city of Birmingham, Alabama, have "signed on" to the program. As of early 2008, over 600,000 computers had been distributed, though (for example) Brazil alone has requested nearly double that number. Negroponte announced in spring 2008, that Microsoft would be a provider to OLPC, precipitating the departure of several staff.

[2] http://www.linux.org/info/linux_govt.html

- Munich, Germany
- The Government of Japan
- Junta de Extramadura, Spain
- Vienna, Austria
- Bergen, Norway
- Largo, Florida, USA
- Pinellas County, Florida, USA
- Bloomington, Monroe County, Indiana, USA
- United States Postal Service
- Administrative Office of the U.S. Courts
- The Federal Government of Brazil
- Mexico City, Mexico
- National Security Agency, USA
  (known as Security Enhanced Linux or SE Linux)
- Department of Human Services, New Jersey, USA
- The State of Nebraska, USA
- United States Census Bureau
- Federal Bureau of Investigation (FBI), USA
- National Aeronautics and Space Administration (NASA), USA
- State of Mississippi, USA
- Ministry of Information and Communication, South Korea
- The Government of Venezuela
- Central Scotland Police, UK
- Centrelink, Australia
- Ministry of Finance, Denmark
- United States Navy
- Northern Territory, Australia
- Army of the People's Republic of China

This is quite impressive. In fact, since the farcical resolution meeting concerning OOXML, several governments (e.g. the Netherlands and Uruguay) have endorsed/adopted ODF. Multiple standards are not new. But they waste time and energy. The techies will determine what is going to be used, anyway. As pointed out earlier, there are no conforming implementations where OOXML is concerned. Standardization prior to implementation is insane.

Here's an example of just that.

In 1977 the British Standards Institute proposed to ISO that a standard architecture was needed to define the communications infrastructure. ISO set up a subcommittee of a technical committee to consider this (ISO/TC 97/SC 16). The next year ISO published its "Provisional Model of Open Systems Architecture (ISO/TC 97/SC 16 N 34). This was labeled "Reference Model" and called OSIRM (or, by Mike Padlipsky and his colleagues "ISORM" — pronounced "eye-sorm"). It was based on work at Honeywell which had been derived from IBM's Systems Network Architecture (SNA).[3] The ANSI immediately accepted the submission (it was the only one) and forwarded it to ISO. The US Government dutifully required it until 1994, when it recognized the de facto use of TCP, which nearly every network worldwide had been using for over a decade.

All of this has come about thanks to the Internet/Web. According to Gregory Clark (*A Farewell to Alms*, 2007), the speed at which information traveled over the two millennia prior to the 19th century was about one mile per hour. Then came telegraphy, telephony, and the Internet. In 2008, information travels at just under the speed of light.

The result is that not only code, but "comments" are known virtually instantly. Thus, while it might have taken a long time for information to cross the Atlantic two centuries ago[4], I now

---

[3]I am not going to exhaust you with the whole tale, which can be found in my *Casting the Net*, chapter 13.

[4]The Battle of New Orleans took place on January 8, 1815, and was the final

receive "same day service." There is an echoic effect here: we not only know what's new (and are able to download it) but we know about talks, promises, press releases and other FUD methodologies rapidly — and thousands of rebuttals and refutations are visible equally rapidly.

For instance, from OpenForum Europe:[5]

> An independent report published today examines the special status enjoyed by ECMA International in the world of international standardisation and severely criticises the role that this consortium has played in ISO's recent process relating to Microsoft's Office Open XML (OOXML). The report is part of a series of whitepapers on ICT Standardisation published by the specialist firm 79 Brinkburn. The report which is entirely independent of any third party, and is without sponsorship, reviews the position that ECMA International plays in international standardisation, in particular in light of their support for the fast track of OOXML through ISO. The report is blunt in its criticism and will doubtless be seized on as one further piece of evidence that demolishes the transparency and independence of the said process.
>
> The report applies the Brinkburn Analysis to evaluate the validity of ECMA's privileged status within ISO, one not enjoyed by any other Consortia, and criticises ECMA for having "virtually no representation for many points of view" and "no outreach and no liasons with other consortia". Most damning of all is the conclusion in respect of OOXML — "It is a breach, almost, of common sense. ECMA, through

---

major battle of the War of 1812. The Treaty of Ghent had been signed on 24 December 1814, but news didn't not reach New Orleans until February.

[5]http://www.openforumeurope.org/press-room/press-releases/ new-report-critical-of-ecma-s-role-in-standardisation-of-ooxml/ (2008–04– 17)

its members, has created, with the exploitation of a loophole, a precedent that may well enable the breakdown of the formal standards process".

Or from a blog entry from Harvey Anderson, VP and General Counsel, Mozilla Corporation:[6]

> We've just begun a new project at Mozilla to create a tool that can help defend against invalid software patents. The project is currently sponsored by Mozilla and Emily Berger of the EFF. The problem is that when patents are asserted or enforced, it's difficult, expensive, and time consuming to find the references (documents or other software/systems) that contain the elements of the asserted patent claims, also known as prior art. Finding prior art is often one of the key defenses to claims of patent infringement; however, this part of the process is archaic, subjective, resource intensive, and inefficient ....
>
> Our goal is to spec out the project, build a beta and see if it works. If it does, we'll extend and enhance, if not, we'll try something else. The details of the project are at: http://wiki.mozilla.org/Legal:Prior_ Art#Summary.

I haven't discussed the EFF (Electronic Frontier Foundation) earlier, but it is of great importance. Founded in 1990 in response to the Steve Jackson Games raid by the US Secret Service, the EFF began from a small group:

> In an electronic community called the Whole Earth 'Lectronic Link (now WELL.com) several informed technologists understood exactly what civil liberties issues were involved. Mitch Kapor, former president of Lotus Development Corporation, John Perry

---

[6]http://lockshot.wordpress.com/ (2008–04–21)

Barlow, Wyoming cattle rancher and lyricist for the Grateful Dead, and John Gilmore, an early employee of Sun Microsystems, decided to do something about it. They formed an organization to work on civil liberties issues raised by new technologies. And on the day they formally announced the organization, they announced that they were representing Steve Jackson Games and several of the company's bulletin board users in a lawsuit they were bringing against the United States Secret Service. The Electronic Frontier Foundation was born!

The Steve Jackson Games case turned out to be an extremely important one in the development of a proper legal framework for cyberspace. For the first time, a court held that electronic mail deserves at least as much protection as telephone calls. We take for granted today that law enforcement must have a warrant that particularly describes all electronic mail messages before seizing and reading them. The Steve Jackson Games case established that principle.[7]

While the EFF has continued to press forward, about five years ago, Dan Ravicher and Eben Moglen (both founders of the Software Freedom Law Center) together with Brian Kahin and Arti K. Rai formed the Public Patent Foundation, or PUBPAT, seeking to limit abuse of the US patent system. Among other things, they have been effective where the Pfizer Lipitor Patent, the Microsoft FAT patent, the Columbia Cotransformation Patent, the Forgent Networks JPEG Related Patent and the Monsanto patents related to genetically modified crops were concerned: all of these have been reversed.[8]

Blogs like Groklaw[9] further spread information and awareness. Groklaw is an award-winning website that covers legal

---

[7]http://www.eff.org/about/history
[8]http://www.pubpat.org/index.htm
[9]http://www.groklaw.net/

news of interest to the free and open-source software community. Issues covered include the SCO-Linux lawsuits, the EU anti-trust case against Microsoft, and the Office Open XML application to ISO. (An early version of the first chapters of this book was posted there.) Groklaw, which has won many awards since its beginnings in 2003, is the personal creation of one person, Pamela Jones. But the blog has thousands of contributors and tens of thousands of readers. And they are truly international. I have seen contributions from North and South America, Asia, Australia, and Europe.

The EFF, PUBPAT, Groklaw and others are like a bright light, causing entities like Microsoft to scuttle away and forcing them to attempt throwing up defenses. But exposing FUD and base activities destroys them.

As a final example, Microsoft has long claimed "thousands" of patents on protocols and functionality. Bob Muglia, a Microsoft executive, had said "For commercial distribution, Microsoft will license related patents on reasonable and non-discriminatory terms, at low royalty rates." He was referring to the nearly 45,000 pages of "protocol documentation" Microsoft had released in February and March of 2008. But, when Jason Perlow of ZDNet asked Tom Kemp exactly what Microsoft might be referring to, the response was surprising. Kemp is President and Chief Executive Officer at Centrify, and has spent a lot of time analyzing the lists and checking Microsoft's patents.

He told Perlow that "roughly 80 percent of Microsoft's server protocols do not appear [to] have patents filed or patents assigned in the United States .... It seems that the majority of patented protocols stem from Microsoft's Active Directory Replication, which has 10 patents assigned to it in and of itself — roughly 20% of all the server protocols, and another 4 are assigned just for DCOM."[10]

But Microsoft's war on Linux is unwinnable, like "a land war in Asia." As *RoughlyDrafted* put it: "As Microsoft begins

<hr>

[10]http://blogs.zdnet.com/BTL/?p=8562

The Daemon, the Gnu, and the Penguin

waging its all out war against Linux, how far will its popularity decline? And will that war be conveniently limited to a far away land, or might it cause fear and distress to Microsoft's own customers? Would Microsoft's own customers be targeted as potential enemies in massive, RIAA-style crackdowns?"[11]

Fortune Magazine asked whether Microsoft would ever seek to "sue its customers for royalties, the way the record industry has," Microsoft CEO Steve Ballmer replied, "That's not a bridge we've crossed, and not a bridge I want to cross today on the phone with you."

Sue your own customers? They must be nuts.

Openness.

Speed of Communication.

Community.

---

[11]http://www.roughlydrafted.com/RD/RDM.Tech.Q2.07/
878F362F-2BF5-4C86-84E7-9C976F7BDDD4.html
    I'd like to thank Daniel Eran Dilger for permission to use his Roughly-Drafted material.

30 Are We There Yet?

Vint Cerf has remarked: "People are inventing not only virtual places but new economic principles."

Law professor Yochai Benkler (Harvard) explains how collaborative projects like Wikipedia and Linux represent the next stage of human organization. By disrupting traditional economic production, copyright law and established competition, they're paving the way for a new set of economic laws, where empowered individuals are put on a level playing field with industry giants.

In his *The Wealth of Networks* (2006), Benkler argues that blogs and other modes of participatory communication can lead to "a more critical and self-reflective culture," where citizens are empowered by the ability to publicize their own opinions on a range of issues. Benkler raises the possibility that a culture where information was shared freely could prove more efficient economically than one where innovation is too-frequently protected by patent or copyright law, since the marginal cost of re-producing most information is effectively nothing.

This is the thread that Clay Shirky elaborates upon in his *Here Comes Everybody*[1]. Let's look at the economics more closely . . .

Ryan Paul, Ars Technica's open source journalist, has posted a report indicating that:

> The Standish Group recently completed an extensive study that examines factors influencing open-source adoption. Based on five years of research and analysis, the report provides intriguing insights into open-

---

[1] (2008; ISBN 1594201536).

source adoption levels and the way that open source is reshaping the software industry. Individuals who participated in the Standish survey identified several key drivers for open source adoption, including lower costs, better security and reliability, and faster development speed ....

Over 70 percent said that Red Hat Linux is less vulnerable to security issues than Microsoft's operating system.[2]

The identification of Red Hat is unimportant.
Paul's article concludes:

Despite adoption challenges, the Standish report concludes that open source software is a big win for businesses, which are saving billions and passing that savings along to consumers. "Open source dominates web server installations and is an integral part of most e-commerce websites," the report says. "The open-source movement is advancing because of feature-rich, secure, high-quality, reliable software with compelling economic benefits."

It's worth looking at that Standish report more closely. In an article posted in late April 2008, technology writer Martin Broersma wrote:

Open source software is successfully displacing proprietary applications in many large companies and eating into the annual revenues of proprietary software vendors by $60bn per year, according to research.

According to the study from the Standish Group called Trends in Open Source, released this week, the

[2]http://arstechnica.com/news.ars/post/
20080425-study-70-percent-say-red-hat-more-secure-than-windows.html

losses of proprietary software makers are dispropor-
tionate to the actual spend on open source software,
which is a mere six per cent of an estimated worldwide spend of $1tr per year. The researchers put
this difference down to the fact a large proportion of
open source isn't paid for — an intended result of
the open source licensing structure ....

The study, the result of five years of research, states
if open source products and services were calculated
at commercial prices, open source as a whole would
be equivalent to the largest software company in
the world, with revenues exceeding the combined
income of Microsoft, Oracle and Computer Associates.[3]

And that's it. Open source is a big win. The news media
hammer away at Microsoft's near-monopoly on the desktop. But
that "near-monopoly" is ephemeral. In search engines, Microsoft
barely exists where Google or Yahoo! dominate. Where accuracy
and reliability are required, we find Linux.

In Formula One auto racing, for example, Jonathan Neale, the
managing director of McLaren Racing, says: "Formula One is
a product excellence business that's all about innovation and
technology. We're competing for first place in an environment
where the difference between first and tenth is about 0.6 seconds,
so we're constantly seeking fractions of a second in performance
improvement.

"On average we'll make a change to the car every 20 minutes
during the course of a season, and to do that, simulation is
vital in making efficient changes to the car." Back in the factory,
McLaren uses computational fluid dynamics (CFD) analysis

---

[3]http://software.silicon.com/os/0,39024651,39201838,00.htm

running on Linux on SGI Altix high performance computers to simulate and predict the car's behaviour."[4]

Microsoft is no longer running the industry as they once did. People don't talk about a new release of MS-Office with great anticipation ... they talk about the coolest new web site, blog, or a web-powered app. And millions play free and open source games. (The Wikipedia listed over 500 in mid-2008.)

Open Source has gone from being this hippy/weird/bad thing that CIOs resist, to an accepted part of the IT ecosystem. For example, nobody questions using ISC BIND or DHCP, and when a dot-com starts up they build a cluster of Linux boxes, not Windows servers. (Not to mention that Firefox is a major force now ... and has an economic model that makes it self-funding).

In fact, it may well be "game over" for old-school corporations like Microsoft.

When Microsoft launched its bid for Yahoo, John Markoff wrote:

> Founded in 1975, Microsoft has had a longer run than most tech companies largely because it became very good at chasing the next big thing: an operating system, point-and-click computing, software for servers, Web services, video games, and, most recently, Internet search and online advertising.
>
> Technological innovation may not have always been what gave Microsoft the edge. It has been frequently criticized for me-tooism and for getting it right the third time. Sometimes, marketing skill and bullying seemed also to be keys to its success. (To be fair, the creative use of those skills can also be regarded as a form of innovation.)
>
> Microsoft won huge business battles, starting with its domination of personal-computer software against

---

[4]http://www.itpro.co.uk/applications/features/192522/
linux-and-formula-one.html

Apple during the 1980s. A decade later, it made quick work of Netscape Communications, which popularized Web browsing in the mid-1990s.

While Microsoft remains very profitable because of its lock on desktop software, its efforts to dislodge the Valley's leading third-generation Internet company, Google, have so far failed.

Google's central innovation, Internet search, has confounded Microsoft, despite investing billions in both technology development and numerous smaller acquisitions. Internet technology has overtaken the PC desktop as the center of the action, as people increasingly view the computer as merely a doorway to their virtual world. Google calls this phenomenon "cloud computing."[5]

He had earlier noted, "In moving to buy Yahoo, Microsoft may be firing the final shot of yesterday's war." This, of course, is because Microsoft "embraces" and "engulfs" only to extinguish. It has lost where search engines are concerned; and (as of 2 May 2008) it has "withdrawn" its bid for Yahoo!.[6]

On a historical note, Julius Caesar was assassinated in 44 BCE. Rome was besieged, overrun and sacked by Alaric in 410 AD. There were nearly five centuries of decline. It won't take that long for the Microsoft empire to collapse, but it certainly won't be rapid.

---

[5] http://www.nytimes.com/2008/02/03/technology/03valley.html?
pagewanted=all

[6] It's hard to anticipate exactly what this means: perhaps Microsoft thinks it can pressure Yahoo!'s stockholders into considering a buyout; perhaps, Microsoft has decided to go after smaller fish; perhaps this is a ruse to drive Yahoo!'s stock price down, so that it can be bought more cheaply. Billionaire Carl Icahn is on Microsoft's side, and wants to oust Yahoo!'s board. But Microsoft may be too arrogant. A sneaky trick will reawaken the European Union, and might even rouse the US Department of Justice, unlikely as that may appear.

Microsoft repeatedly shoots itself in the foot (Vista is a great example); free and open source systems, applications and games offer so much variety, that their luxurious growth overwhelms inferior "new" products.

Moreover, despite the assertion by Christopher P. Liddell, Microsoft's chief financial officer, that "There are no Vista-related issues at all," the monolith is having problems. "Sales in the segment [of Microsoft] that sells the Office productivity suite and other business applications edged down 2 per cent to $4.75 billion US from a year ago"[7] yet "researcher IDC showed PC sales exceeded forecasts in the quarter. PC shipments rose 15 percent."

An anonymous blogger posted this version of the next few years:

- Microsoft gets fixated on Yahoo, and ignores the rest of their business.

- The battle is long and hard, but Yahoo eventually merges with some other company, foiling Microsoft's bid.

- Meanwhile, Microsoft rushes out "Windows 7", which ends up being little more than Vista Service Pack 2.

- Windows 7 is another flop.

- The Microsoft executive offices turn into a battle ground, with everyone blaming everyone else for the disaster.

- By the time things settle down, Microsoft's OS and office software have declined to 60% market share, and it's a whole new world in the computer industry.

I'm not at all certain that I agree with all of this, but the last four items are extremely likely.

---

[7] http://www.cbc.ca/technology/story/2008/04/24/microsoftprofit.html

Comparisons with other segments of the economy are valuable. If one looks at the automobile industry, for example, in 1985, 1,530,410 "new vehicles" were sold in Canada. In 2005, there were 1,630,310. However, in 1985, 794,965 were passenger vehicles manufactured in North America, whereas in 2005, there were 574,639.[8] So, while sales were up by 6.5%, sales of North American manufactures were down by nearly 28%. Looked at from the viewpoint of the US Department of Commerce, GM's share, 36% in 1990, stands at 26% in 2007. Ford's 1990 share, 24%, is now 17%.

This is the fate I imagine Microsoft, the prime example of closed, proprietary software, paralleling. The 'long tail' for Microsoft will be their waning business, a very different sort of "long tail" from that used by Amazon or written about by Anderson.

We are now in a very different world from the one we were in but a few decades ago. Where towns and their surrounding farms formed near-isolates. National networks in television and, more recently, the internet, have destroyed that isolation. The news of an earthquake or a tsunami moves around the planet at near the speed of light. A tennis victory or a medical breakthrough become known just as rapidly.

It has been pointed out that "to many eyes, all bugs are shallow." That's one of the reasons that free and open source works — not that the systems or applications are bug-free, but that because they are open, they can be ameliorated rapidly. Similarly, as hardware or demand change, FOSS (free and open source software) can change rapidly as well. A dinosaur can't change direction rapidly.

After MakerFaire 2008, the Institute for the Future distributed its "Future of Making Map." The first point of which ran:

> Many of the best ideas may come from unexpected
> contributors, including those who are so far outside

---

[8]http://www.statcan.ca/english/freepub/63-007-XIE/2008002/t015_en.htm

the organization's own walls that they speak a different language. To succeed in the future, organizations will need to look to both internal and external sources of innovation. Seeking an outside-in perspective on internal challenges may require long-held processes to be rethought, from the design cycle to R&D budgets to intellectual property strategies. Once open to the idea of a networked organization, it's relatively easy to identify and engage with external networks of exceptional people through community R&D platforms such as Instructables, InnoCentive, and Nine-Sigma.[9]

While it is hard to translate others' words, I read "a different language" to include the language of cooperation as opposed to that of hierarchic direction. Again, the enormous monolith has problems of agility.

Volunteerism and cooperativism have combined with rapid communication to produce the world of free and open software we see today. Just as General Motors and Ford have found it more difficult to adapt than the Asian automotive companies, so too the massive software entities are succumbing to adaptable entities.

Let me give the last words to Donald Knuth, one of the great programmers and an undercredited father of open source.

The success of open source code is perhaps the only thing in the computer field that hasn't surprised me during the past several decades. But it still hasn't reached its full potential; I believe that open-source programs will begin to be completely dominant as the economy moves more and more from products towards services, and as more and more volunteers arise to improve the code. For example, open-source

---

[9]http://iftf.org/node/1766ring

code can produce thousands of binaries, tuned perfectly to the configurations of individual users, whereas commercial software usually will exist in only a few versions. A generic binary executable file must include things like inefficient "sync" instructions that are totally inappropriate for many installations; such wastage goes away when the source code is highly configurable. This should be a huge win for open source.[10]

"The animation and FX for Indiana Jones and the Kingdom of the Crystal Skull; Star Wars: The Clone Wars; WALL-E; 300; The Golden Compass; Harry Potter and the Order of the Phoenix; and I Am Legend, to name but a few recent movies, were all created using Pixar's RenderMan and Autodesk Maya running on Linux clusters." — Steven J. Vaughan-Nichols, ComputerWorld, 18 August 2008.

---

[10]http://www.informit.com/articles/article.aspx?p=1193856 (Born in 1938, Knuth has been given the Turing Award [1974], the Von Neumann Medal [1995] and the Kyoto Prize [1996]. He is a brilliant author with an extraordinary range of interests.)

Index

Novell, 65, 76, 77, 83, 125, 131

O'Brien, Mike, 23, 25
O'Dell, Mike, 18, 62
O'Donnell, Ciaran, 87
O'Reilly, Tim, 156
ODF, *see* Open Document Format
Office Open XML, 158, 163, 164
Offmyserver, 95
OLPC, *see* One Laptop per Child
Olsen, Ken, 1, 8, 53, 64
Olson, James E., 64
One Laptop per Child, 161
OOXML, *see* Office Open XML
open architecture, 53
Open Document Format, 158, 163
Open Group, 65, 76
Open Software Foundation, 64, 65
open source, 70, 102, 132, 139, 153–156, 170–172, 175, 176
OpenBSD, 98, 100
OpenExchange, 157
OpenOffice, 158
Orange Book, 99
OS/2, 85
Osborne, Adam, 54
OSF, *see* Open Software Foundation
OSIRM, 163

Packard, Keith, 118
Padlipsky, Mike, 163

Partridge, Craig, 106
patents, 101
Paul, Ryan, 169, 170
PDP-11, 15, 21, 28, 37, 41, 42, 57, 83, 86, 102
Perens, Bruce, 115, 129
Perlow, Jason, 167
Pike, Rob, 79
pirate, 48, 151
Pixar, 129
Plan 9, 79
Plauger, P.J., 59, 85, 86
Polk, Jeff, 74, 93
Presotto, Dave, 79, 80
pride, 155
Prime Time Freeware, 59
Project Athena, 116, 118
Project MAC, 6, 7
public domain, 33
Public Patent Foundation, 166
PUBPAT, *see* Public Patent Foundation, 167
Pugh, E.W., 4

QED, 27
Quarterman, John, 61, 106

Rachiver, Dan, 166
Rai, Arti K., 166
Rashid, Rick, 120
Raymond, Eric, 127, 133, 146, 156
Red Hat, 70, 115, 124, 125, 127, 130–132, 170
Redmond Linux, 130

CPSIA information can be obtained
at www.ICGtesting.com
Printed in the USA
BVHW071923080120
568944BV00004B/259/P